Overcome Social Anxiety

Proven Solutions and Treatments That Cure Social Disorders, Phobias, People-Pleasing, and Shyness. Drastically Improve Your Self Esteem, Build Confidence, and Just Be Yourself

Derick Howell

© **Copyright Derick Howell 2020 - All rights reserved.**

The content contained within this book may not be reproduced, duplicated or transmitted without direct written permission from the author or the publisher.

Under no circumstances will any blame or legal responsibility be held against the publisher, or author, for any damages, reparation, or monetary loss due to the information contained within this book. Either directly or indirectly. You are responsible for your own choices, actions, and results.

Legal Notice:

This book is copyright protected. This book is only for personal use. You cannot amend, distribute, sell, use, quote or paraphrase any part, or the content within this book, without the consent of the author or publisher.

Disclaimer Notice:

Please note the information contained within this document is for educational and entertainment purposes only. All effort has been executed to present accurate, up to date, and reliable, complete information. No warranties of any kind are declared or implied. Readers acknowledge that the author is not engaging in the rendering of legal, financial, medical or professional advice. The content within this book has been derived from various sources. Please consult a licensed professional before attempting any techniques outlined in this book.

By reading this document, the reader agrees that under no circumstances is the author responsible for any losses, direct or indirect, which are incurred as a result of the use of the information contained within this document, including, but not limited to, — errors, omissions, or inaccuracies.

Your Free Gift

This book includes a free bonus booklet. All information on how you can quickly secure your free gift can be found at the end of this book. It may only be available for a limited time.

TABLE OF CONTENTS

INTRODUCTION 1

CHAPTER ONE: 5

    What is Social Anxiety?

CHAPTER TWO: 17

    Why Do People Get Socially Anxious?

CHAPTER THREE: 31

    Tips for Dealing with Social Anxiety

CHAPTER FOUR: 41

    Overcoming Social Anxiety

CHAPTER FIVE: 51

    Relaxation Techniques

CHAPTER SIX: 63

    Stop People-Pleasing

CHAPTER SEVEN: 73

    Cure Your Shyness

CHAPTER EIGHT: 81

    How to Build Social Confidence

CHAPTER NINE: 89

    Improving Your Self Esteem

CHAPTER TEN: 97

    Therapy for Social Anxiety

FINAL WORDS 105
RESOURCES 109
YOUR FREE GIFT 111

INTRODUCTION

Have you ever prepared so much for a presentation only to get there and just freeze up or stutter through your talk? You've probably also felt that mild uneasiness that comes with talking to strangers, right? It may be normal to feel a bit nervous in social situations, but if your everyday interactions are causing you fear, embarrassment, self-consciousness, and significant anxiety, then you have what is called social anxiety – a disorder that can ruin your life if you don't overcome it.

There are differing degrees of social anxiety, but, all in all, it can make us act awkwardly in any social situation. Social anxiety disorder is a mental health condition that makes people feel irrational anxiety whenever they interact socially. For these people, interaction with others is very fearful; they are mostly scared or anxious about being evaluated or judged negatively. If not kept in check, it can create fear in almost every area of one's life, amongst other things. It also causes low self-esteem, depression, negative thoughts, heightened sensitivity to criticism, and poor social skills.

Social anxiety is very prevalent. Some people have even concluded that it is just the way they are, and they can't do anything about it, but that is not correct. The difference between those who overcome social anxiety and those who live with it is that the former did something about it, and the other chose to resign to their fate.

In a broad sense, it is okay to be shy; most of us can be shy to varying degrees. But if your level of shyness is high enough to deter you from living your best life, then it is abnormal, and something needs to be done about it. Because if you think of it, nothing that is within your power to change should hamper your progress in life. Nothing within your control should stop you from living your best life.

Social anxiety can cause you to blow a career opportunity, ruin that presentation you've prepared so much for, or freeze up on a date and go home wondering what went wrong. If you have ever been in any of these situations, you are not alone. Millions of Americans are with you on this. The good news is you can do something about it, and reading this book is taking a step in the right direction.

There are various treatments and steps, as well as lifestyle and mindset changes you can take to get over your fear of social interactions. Social anxiety is a thing of the mind, and that is where we must go if we wish to overcome it. While therapies that work to adjust the mindset, such as Cognitive Behavioral Therapy (CBT), have proven to be effective against social anxiety, lifestyle changes such as reducing stress, exercising more, participating in social events, getting enough sleep, and eating healthier are also good ways of handling social anxiety. In the course of this book, we will take an in-depth look into the different ways that can help you reclaim your life from the chilly grip of social anxiety.

I know these methods will prove effective for you, because as a professional speaker and an anxiety coach who has helped several people with social anxiety, and after having suffered from it myself, I can say that I know what works (and what doesn't). I have presented on the topic multiple times and written several pieces to help people with a social anxiety disorder. I am particularly passionate about this subject because it nearly robbed me of my dreams, and when I successfully moved past it, I was on the right path again. That freedom I felt after breaking free is my motivation, and I hope that before you flip the last page of this book, you too will experience that freedom.

Why should you aim for this freedom? You should do so for everything. The benefits are so numerous, and I can attest to that from firsthand experience. When you eventually rid yourself of social anxiety disorder, you will finally get the chance to:

- Be yourself
- Socialize more
- Gain more friends
- Be more comfortable in public
- Increase your self-esteem
- Experience freedom from excruciating thoughts
- Experience freedom from extreme sensitivity
- And more...

How do I know this? I used to experience terrible fear whenever I would go on stage to talk, or when meeting new people, or countless other social settings - but the tips in this book have been the most beneficial for me, and that has helped me get over my fears and anxiety. Now, I am a well-established speaker and writer who has managed to make a name for myself. I have also succeeded in building successful relationships that have kept my emotional and business life in good shape. I socialize very well and enjoy life. You're probably wondering if I also have good self-esteem? You sure can bet on that.

However, don't be fooled. I did not achieve these dramatic results by simply being extraordinary. It is not just me, as millions of Americans are waking up to reality and ridding themselves of this burden. I've watched people under my mentorship go from extremely timid and shy to daring and outgoing. You can be next!

What am I promising to you? After reading this book, you will overcome social anxiety (that, I am sure of). I will not hold back anything from you as I will dole out every step, system, and hack that has worked for me and countless others, and I will provide you with actionable steps to help you get over your social anxiety in no time.

You can start facing your fears and getting over your social anxiety as soon as you start reading this book. With every single minute, you are held up with social anxiety; you let opportunities pass you by. Remember that the future belongs to those who act now. All it takes is for you to read this book, follow the action steps outlined within, and you will see drastic changes unfold in your life.

Continue reading to find out the secrets that have helped me and countless others get over the worst of social anxiety. Don't just read this book; make a decision to follow every step I have included. Two people might read this book and experience differing impacts. The hungrier you are for results, the faster you will get them with this book.

CHAPTER ONE:

What is Social Anxiety?

The term social anxiety is often confused with shyness, but they are two totally different things. The nervousness and uncomfortable feeling that comes with a social event is social anxiety. In this section, I will give you a detailed explanation of what social anxiety is. My aim of doing this is to help you understand what social anxiety is, the different ways it can affect you, why it affects you, when it happens, what triggers it, and what it feels like when it is happening. I believe that when you have understood these aspects, then you can be better prepared to handle the anxiety more effectively. So, let's explore together.

So, What Really Is Social Anxiety?

Social anxiety is the extreme fear of having a negative evaluation by other people. People with this disorder are always on edge when they are around people because they fear that they might embarrass themselves. The fear is stemming from the fact that they just don't feel good enough about themselves. As if that was not enough, they still fear that they may be judged for showing signs that suggest they are anxious, such as sweating, trembling, or blushing. The problem can easily snowball.

To escape this maze of anxiety, people with social anxiety often keep to themselves and avoid social gatherings. But the problem with this decision is that social gatherings are inescapable. Think of the classroom, job interviews, group conversions, parties, balls, events, beaches, cinemas... they all scream "social gathering." So if you must avoid "social gatherings" you are indirectly avoiding life.

This reminds me of when I was in school. I would refuse to raise my hand to answer a question in class, even when I knew the answer. The few times I tried, it didn't end well, as I made such a mess of myself that I could not even look my mates in the eyes after class. So I decided, I'm just going to stay silent in class. Do you know what that cost me? It caused me to not have a good relationship with any of my teachers because I doubt they ever noticed me in class. Less bright students went on to build lasting relationships with those professors, and sometimes it even showed in their grades. Not that the professors were biased, but being close to a professor will inspire you to work harder and score better grades to impress them.

Occurrence

If you have experienced the symptoms of this disorder, don't think it is just you. It is not just you. According to the 2017 statistics from the National Institute of Mental Health, about 7% of people in the United States have suffered social anxiety over the last year. And of the rest, another 12% will suffer social anxiety at some point in their lives.

Types of Social Anxiety Disorder

According to the Diagnostic and Statistical Manual of Mental Disorders (DSM-5), there are two categories of SAD. These categories are Generalized Social Anxiety and Performance-Only Social Anxiety. Before now, it was known as generalized SAD and specific SAD. The specific was replaced with "performance-only" since the "specific" was originally referring to when a patient suffers anxiety when performing.

Let's take a brief look at the two categories:

Generalized Social Anxiety

This refers to the category of people who experience fear and anxiety in both performance and social settings. This disorder is considered to be more serious than performance-only SAD because it is not selective, and it is experienced more frequently. According to the DSM-5, sufferers of Generalized social anxiety experience fear and anxiety when:

1. Exposed to unfamiliar people and prone to scrutiny
2. Scared of possible humiliation

In mild cases, people with generalized social anxiety can be comfortable with their close friends and families.

Performance-Only Social Anxiety

As the name suggests, people with this disorder will only feel fear and anxiety when they are in a performance situation. To demonstrate this, one can experience no anxiety in social gatherings but become anxious when it is time to perform before a group of people. Performance can be an art or a speech.

If you have this form of SAD, don't celebrate yet; it can still hold you back in its right. This form of SAD can greatly hamper your hopes of progressing in your career or other performance-based achievements.

Aside from when they feel their anxiety, there are other differences between the two categories of SAD. The differences are in their method of treatment, response to treatment, physical symptoms during an attack, and the age they were when they first experienced anxiety.

You need to know the type of disorder you have before progressing to the cure section of this book. This is an ideal time for you to conduct a self-check and be completely truthful to yourself on where and when you get anxious, so you can know how to properly apply the techniques and steps I will be sharing with you in the latter chapters of this book. It is usually best to adapt treatment methods that are tailored for a specific condition to get the appropriate result.

Knowing If You Have Social Anxiety Disorder

At first, some people make the mistake of thinking their symptoms are a result of a non-psychiatric medical condition. Start by eliminating this line of thought. You can do this by ensuring that you are not suffering from anxiety for other medical reasons such as hyperthyroidism, endocrine problems, certain heart problems, or low blood sugar. You can have a health care provider evaluate your condition.

Can it Lead to Other Complications?

Social anxiety disorder, just like other serious health conditions, can have complications. The most common one is its persistence throughout a person's lifetime. If you don't do anything about it, it can stay with you throughout your life. Most people erroneously believe that when they grow older, they will outgrow their anxiety. I hate to break it to you... but it doesn't work that way. Rather, it gathers momentum as you grow older.

Negative self-talk and trouble being assertive are also some signs of extreme social anxiety.

In some severe cases, the sufferer might choose to drop out of school, or quit work, or go into isolation. If this happens, and it is not checked, depression, and even suicidal thoughts, may follow. Unchecked social anxiety has even driven some to cut their lives short.

More specific complications that could arise are:

Comorbidity

Comorbidity is a concept in medicine in which other conditions coexist with the condition in focus. Social anxiety is also comorbid. Statistics tell us 66% of patients suffering from SAD are also suffering from other related mental illnesses. Some of the common illnesses it coexists with are clinical depression, anxiety disorders, and avoidant personality disorder. Experts say SAD patients are likely to develop clinical depression because they lack personal relationships and keep to themselves most of the time. A publication from the National Center for Biotechnology Information has found that people with SAD are 1.49 to 3.5 times more likely to have clinical depression, too.

Substance Abuse

Since depression and anxiety are often too much for people with SAD, they may start seeking something to let them "self medicate," that they believe will help their condition. That is where substance abuse comes in. Statistics have it that 20% of people with SAD are also alcohol dependent.

And how well do they fare when they start depending on substances? They become even worse. It has been discovered that socially anxious people who depend on substances are less likely to try group-based treatments.

Key Insight

Some socially anxious people are aware that their anxiety is misplaced; they know it is uncalled for. Sometimes, they even demand an answer from themselves as to why they are allowing such a minute issue to bother them so much. But then, their anxious feelings persist and continue escalating. So, knowing you are socially anxious isn't total freedom, but it's a good step in the right direction. You will need to seek a real solution like the ones discussed in this book to set yourself free. No matter how chronic your social anxiety is, it is curable, and there is hope for you.

What Social Anxiety Is Not

Social anxiety is often confused with many other things. Below, we'll look at some of the things we experience (that may make us believe we have social anxiety) to give us a better understanding of what it is.

It is not "Stage Fright"

We all know that stage fright is a very common phenomenon among humans. Most people will feel nervous if they must stand before a crowd and speak. If that is what you are feeling, it is normal. You are getting that feeling because you are not used to the crowd. You could try enrolling in a speech club that would give you the opportunity to try to talk to a group of people.

Also, most people can feel slightly nervous when attending a social event or taking part in a competition. I will not classify that as a social anxiety disorder. It becomes SAD when you experience excessive fear and anxiety with everyday social events. You are more self-conscious, and you fear embarrassment even when nothing is embarrassing about you.

A person that experiences stage fright will feel comfortable with everyday tasks, such as eating outside or filling out forms in the presence of people, but you may have SAD when these trivial events cause you anxiety.

It is not a Panic Disorder

Due to the nature of social anxiety, people tend to confuse it with panic disorders. Even though they are both in the five major anxiety disorders that are listed in the DSM-5, they still differ in many ways.

The difference is that socially anxious people do not experience panic attacks. What they may experience are anxiety attacks. People with a panic disorder may not realize that it is panic that they are feeling. But people with social anxiety understand that what they are experiencing are fear and anxiety. A person with a panic disorder may even need to visit the hospital after an attack because they may think there is something physically wrong with them, but it is not so for people with social anxiety.

Diagnosis

Sometimes, it can be difficult to tell for sure whether what you have is SAD or not. The best way to know is to check with a doctor or healthcare professional. They can carry out a physical evaluation and basic psychiatric examination. In the physical examination phase, the doctor aims to see if there could be any other physical causes for the way you are feeling. If they ascertain that there is no physical explanation for your condition, they may recommend a psychiatric examination. A psychiatrist or a psychologist will ask you for the symptoms you have experienced, when you experienced them, how often you experience them, and for how long you've been having the symptoms. Some of them will require you to fill out a questionnaire to help with your evaluation.

With SAD, your examiner will always want to find out if the anxiety you feel is so intense that it can interfere with your daily life. Because, as I said earlier, mild anxiety can be normal. He will check if your anxiety can interfere with your career, relationships, or other social concepts.

The mental practitioner is not quick to label you with SAD. He must go through due process. In fact, in the U.S and some other countries, the symptoms you describe must agree with the criteria stated in the Diagnostic and Statistical Manual (DSM) for social anxiety.

Unlike other categories of medical conditions, mental conditions cannot be verified in a lab test. So it will be judged based on some predetermined criteria. In the case of SAD, the criteria are published in a handbook known as the Diagnostic and Statistical Manual of Mental Disorders. It is published by the American Psychiatric Association (APA).

SAD Diagnostic Criteria

Now let's look at the criteria as outlined in the Diagnostic and Statistical Manual of Mental Disorders:

- The patient fears any social situation that can make him the focal point, such as public speaking, eating outside, or meeting new people.
- The patient has a marked fear of humiliating or embarrassing himself or getting rejected by people because of his actions or his symptoms of anxiety.
- The patient experiences fear or anxiety that is not proportional to the threat.
- The patient has experienced this condition for 6 months or longer.
- Due to the fear, the patient experiences significant distress or impairment in certain areas of his life, such as career, school, or relationship.
- The fear or anxiety being felt by the patient is not due to the effect of other drugs or medications. The anxiety is not caused by other mental or physical health conditions.
- And if the patient only experiences these fears when they are performing before people, then it is not generalized, it is of the "performance only" category.

Can it be cured?

This condition can be cured using psychotherapy and medication. Let's look at the options available to you.

Psychotherapy

We have established that the anxiety and fear you feel whenever you get those attacks are not real. But you will never see it like that. Those people you think don't like you? The truth is that they do. These incorrect assumptions you hold about yourself are not true. To help you see these things for what they are, psychological treatments will use several established techniques that will expose the truth about your problems. It is not going to happen all of a sudden; it will be a gradual process. But when it is done, you will be able to cope with those symptoms and overcome them eventually.

One very important therapy that has proven very effective against social anxiety is Cognitive Behavioral Therapy (CBT). I will show you how you can use this therapy to overcome social anxiety later in this book. Other therapies, such as interpersonal therapy and family therapy, can also be used for handling social anxiety.

CBT is particularly helpful because it will help to keep track of your thought patterns that are responsible for your symptoms. It takes attention away from what other people think about you to what you think about yourself. This is important because it is the way you think about yourself that gives you the symptoms you feel. With CBT, you will learn to identify and modify those negative thoughts that have held you down for a long while now.

Medications

In severe cases of SAD, medication can also be used. Several medications exist for this condition, but the most common is the selective serotonin reuptake inhibitors (SSRIs). They are widely used because people consider it the safest and most effective.

Examples of medications that are based on selective serotonin reuptake inhibitors (SSRIs) are

- Paroxetine (Paxil, Paxil CR)
- Fluvoxamine (Luvox, Luvox CR)
- Sertraline (Zoloft)
- Fluoxetine (Prozac, Sarafem)

This medication can have some side effects on some people. The most common side effects are:

- Headaches
- Nausea
- Insomnia
- Sexual dysfunction

Apart from selective serotonin reuptake inhibitors (SSRIs), other medications that can also be used are Benzodiazepines and beta-blockers.

Benzodiazepines

These are primarily anti-anxiety medications. Common examples are alprazolam (Xanax) and clonazepam (Klonopin). However, due to the addictive nature of these medications, courses are usually kept short to avoid dependence.

The side effects of benzodiazepines may include:

- Confusion
- Loss of balance
- Lightheadedness
- Drowsiness
- Memory loss

Beta-blockers

We know how adrenaline is meant to help us deal with an emergency. In people with social anxiety, it can cause undue anxiety even when there is no emergency. Beta-blockers numb the stimulating effects of adrenaline. But this treatment is not continuous. It is only used for specific situations, such as when you might want to make a presentation.

The suggestions I have provided here are only for informational purposes and shouldn't be substituted for professional medical advice and treatment. Always seek the advice of a therapist or your physician for the medication to use. Never delay or disregard seeking medical advice from a professional because of the information I have provided here.

Now that we have seen social anxiety for what it really is, the next step is to know why people get socially anxious, knowing the root cause will put us in a better position to deal with your SAD accordingly.

In this chapter, you have learned what social anxiety is all about, the meaning, types, criteria for diagnosing the disorder, and possible treatment for it. This aims at introducing you to the concept of Social Anxiety Disorder (SAD). In the next chapter, I will be discussing why people get anxious and the causes of anxiety.

CHAPTER TWO:

Why Do People Get Socially Anxious?

In the first chapter of this book, we took a general look at the subject matter; what is social anxiety? In this chapter, we will be focusing on how, when, and why it affects you. I will be answering some of the common questions you might have on the SAD. Most of the questions you've been secretly asking yourself are answered here, just in case you are not sure if you have a social anxiety disorder. I will leave no stone unturned since I am writing from the abundance of my experience and knowledge. Now, shall we?

When Does It Happen?

Different people with social anxiety disorders may indeed feel it in varying ways, but some certain situations are more likely to trigger it. The following situations are ones that people with this disorder tend to dread the most. And yes, your guess is right, they are all bits of social settings. They include:

- Speaking in public.
- Conversing with strangers.
- Going on dates.
- Making and maintaining eye contact with other people.
- Entering and staying in crowded rooms
- Using restrooms outside.
- Meeting with important people.

- Attending and fielding questions in interviews.
- Partying and being friends.
- Eating in the presence of other people.
- Getting introduced to strangers.
- Being teased.
- Being criticized.
- Going to public places such as school and work.
- Being watched while executing a task.
- Starting conversations with people.
- Declining people's requests.
- Reading aloud.
- Sending texts.

What Does It Feel Like?

Now that we know some of the common triggers, let's look at the most common ways it manifests itself.

1. Feeling Isolated

Look at this statement from an anonymous social anxiety patient

"[Social anxiety] makes me feel as if I am the only one suffering that way, and everyone else is just fine with going out and having a good time together. It makes me feel that no one like me, so why would they want to talk to me? When they do talk to me, I always feel they are trying to find an excuse to get away and go talk to someone else."

From this statement, we can sense a feeling of isolation. It tells you that nobody likes you and nobody wants to be your friend. It makes you feel people don't like you, and they are avoiding you.

2. Erroneous Beliefs

We can see that this condition lies to you. It also paints other people's lives as beds of roses, and only you have to cope with a thorny bed. But in reality, everyone has their fair share of life issues to deal with.

But you likely won't see it like that. Instead, you will see yourself as an unfortunate one.

3. It Freezes Your Reasoning

Another patient narrates his experience by saying:

"Internal' feelings that] include a shakiness in my voice, [and] brain fog that stops me from thinking straight," but also to "physical feelings [that] include an upset stomach, loss of appetite, sweaty hands, muscle stiffness."

This statement captures most of the common symptoms you will find in people with SAD, especially when they are in the midst of people.

What Effects Does it Have on You?

1. Isolation and Depression

Life is more fun and fulfilling when spent with friends, family, and even strangers. But when you let social anxiety close your eyes from seeing this, you just spiral down towards depression. When you experience a problem, you will blow it out of proportion since you will never share it with someone who might help you see it another way.

2. Difficulty with employment and school

People with this disorder always try to choose a path that can help them avoid as many people as possible. The result is a drastic drop in the opportunities available to you. Your intelligence level may be such that you will thrive well in the noble professions such as medicine, engineering, or law, but since you dread interaction, you will not live up to your true potential.

3. Gateway for other sickness

You might not know it yet because maybe you have not gotten to that stage, but social anxiety can open the flood gate for other individual ailments such as substance abuse and life impairment. Because once you slide into depression and do not have any way of socializing, the next thing might be to result in substance abuse, extreme pornography consumption, masturbation, or game addiction. The result is impairment for life.

4. Relationship and family difficulties

The problem here is that people with SAD will convince themselves that nobody wants them, and they will lock out every person who cares about them, and this can spell doom for their relationships. They dread and avoid personal relationships.

5. Low Self-Esteem

People with social anxiety are usually trapped in that feeling of not being good enough. This thought pattern can have destabilizing effects because it will affect the productivity of the sufferer in whatever they do. they will condemn themselves to believe they are second class citizens, and it will show in every aspect of life.

6. Heightened Sensitivity to Criticism

People with social anxiety can easily misinterpret situations, and that makes them easily offended. They can misinterpret constructive criticism that is intended for their own good into something offensive.

Why Do People Get Socially Anxious?

The reason you feel socially anxious might stem from why you became socially anxious in the first place. For example, if you got your anxiety from your first role in that ill-fated drama in high school, then it is very likely that you will get socially anxious whenever you are the center of attention.

This means that two socially anxious people might have different reasons for avoiding a similar situation. But the common reasons fall into the following list:

- Being judged by others in social situations
- Being embarrassed or humiliated
- Accidentally offending someone

- Being the center of attention

What Are You Avoiding?

People with social anxiety disorder have this behavioral problem of avoiding anxiety-provoking situations. As one that is socially anxious, if you anticipate going to a social event, maybe going to a party, you may find yourself getting anxious and decide not to go. Immediately after you choose not to go, you begin to feel your anxiety decreasing and feel more comfortable.

The comfort you feel from the reduction of anxiety after you decide not to go out will only reinforce your avoidance. Now your reward for avoidance is the short-term comfort you feel. This comfort will maintain your fear of negative social situations even when you don't experience embarrassment. For instance, you are lost and trying to find your way, and then you see someone approaching you. You felt so anxious talking to the person and decided not to, and immediately, your anxiety drops. The increase in your anxiety has a lesson attached to it. To either stop talking to people or don't ask for help, in order to feel less anxious. But how long are you going to avoid it?

A crucial element of Cognitive Behavioral Therapy (CBT) is about helping an individual with a social anxiety disorder practice sustainable social situations and to stay in them long enough to learn that nothing bad will happen if they have to speak to a stranger or ask for help. Once this is realized, the anxiety will subside. They also get to learn that being in social situations is something they can do, and their willingness to confront their fears is empowering. After that realization, they will start seeing themselves as the kind of person that can do virtually anything.

What Are the Likely Causes?

According to experts, social anxiety disorders can be traced back to both genetic and environmental causes. All of the cases discussed below are not agreed upon by all, as researchers have differing views on them.

1. **Genetic causes:**

It has been observed that the condition can run in families. If that's the case, some researchers think that genetic links could be a cause of social anxiety, although it is still being researched. This research is attempting to establish just how much of it is hereditary and how much is acquired by individuals.

If your parents or siblings have it, you have a higher risk. I am adding this extra detail so that you can look out for symptoms in your young ones. When detected early, it is easier to manage and cure. If any of your first-degree relatives have SAD, you are 2 to 6 times more likely to suffer from the disorder. (Cuncic 2019)

Several studies have come up with varying heritability rates for SAD, but all of them seem to agree around it falling between 30% to 40%. From this statistic, we can conclude that 1 of every 3 SAD cases can be traced back to genetics. (Concic 2019)

However, scientists have not been able to name the particular genetic makeup that causes SAD. But they have found the chromosomes that are linked with other anxiety disorders like panic attacks and agoraphobia.

2. **Certain chemicals in the body**

With the discovery that wrong levels of serotonin, a brain chemical, an individual may experience heightened sensitivity, scientists are trying to see if there are chemicals in the body that can increase the chances of a social anxiety disorder (SAD).

3. **Neurotransmitters**

Neurotransmitters are the chemical medium through which your brain transmits signals from one cell to another. If there is an imbalance in the levels of this chemical, you can lead to social anxiety disorder.

The common neurotransmitters that have been traced back to anxiety are:

- Norepinephrine
- Dopamine
- Serotonin
- Gamma-aminobutyric acid (GABA)

Psychologists have tested people with a social anxiety disorder, and they discovered that most of them have imbalances in the levels of these neurotransmitters. If we understand how these chemicals interact to bring about anxiety, it could help us in deciding the best medication route to take when attempting to cure the disorder.

4. Brain structure

Then again, some researchers are of the opinion that the amygdala can influence fear response and in some cases, lead to excessive reactions.

Medical researchers are using a technique known as neuroimaging to develop an image of the brain, much the same way x-rays create an image of the inside of our body. They are using this technique to compare blood flow in different areas of the brain that are involved in anxiety, in both phobics and normal people while they are addressing a group of people.

Four areas of the brain are actively involved in anxiety:

i. The brain stem: This part of the brain controls heart rate and breathing. You know how different this can be in socially anxious people.
ii. The limbic system: This part of the brain controls mood and anxiety levels. So if it is faulty, you can experience mood swings and high anxiety levels.
iii. The prefrontal cortex: This part of the brain is responsible for assessing a threat and giving feedback to the brain. If it blows perceived threats out of proportion, you may respond with anxiety.
iv. The motor cortex: This part of the brain is responsible for controlling your muscles.

Using the neuroimaging technique, as we discussed above, scientists studied blood flow in the brain and found some differences with the phobics group when they were addressing a crowd. There was a study in which they used type Positron Emission Tomography (PET), a type of neuroimaging techniques. In the study, they showed that the amygdala, which is a part of the limbic system that controls fear, experienced more blood flow in people with SAD when they were addressing a crowd. (Tillfors et al., 2001).

When they did the same study for people without SAD, they discovered that the cerebral cortex, which was associated with thought, got more blood flow.

1. Weather and demographics:

Some researchers also believe that your location can increase your chances of having SAD. These researchers claim that people in the Mediterranean countries are less likely to have social anxiety disorder when compared to people in Scandinavian countries. They say that warmer weather and higher population density reduce avoidance of social gatherings. And when one goes out often and interacts with people, his chances of suffering from SAD are greatly reduced.

2. Cultural or Societal Factors:

There are still some researchers who believe that cultural factors play a role in reducing social anxiety rates. For instance, if someone is from a culture that encourages communal living, like in traditional African settings, they will have a lesser chance of suffering social anxiety.

On the contrary, if you grew up in a society that emphasizes collectivistic orientation, like Korea and Japan, you have a higher probability of developing social anxiety. For instance, these cultures have a syndrome known as taijin kyofusho. A syndrome centered around the fear of making other people around you uncomfortable (Nagakami et al, 2019).

If you are scared of making people uncomfortable, then that can degenerate into social anxiety. These cultures also emphasize how you fit in.

Risk Factors

Risk factors are the things that can increase your chances of succumbing to social anxiety disorder. In most cases, this disorder starts between early and mid-teenage age, but it can also start earlier than that. At that point, some triggers can heighten the risk of getting the disorder.

Some of the factors are discussed below:

Gender: It has been established that the disorder is more predominant among the female population than the male.

Upbringing: It is also believed that if you grew up witnessing traces of social anxiety with people around you, you could also develop the disorder. So if your parents avoided social gatherings, and they were too protective with you, you can develop the disorder too.

Psychologists believe that fearful and socially anxious parents can transfer both verbal and non-verbal cues that can trigger social anxiety. So if your mum is someone that cares too much about what people will say about her or you, you might grow up being anxious about what people think about you.

Also, as a child, if you were not allowed to go out and socialize very often, you can grow up without developing appropriate social skills. And if any of your parents were particularly critical, overprotective, or rejecting, you can also end up being socially anxious.

Hurtful Childhood Experiences: As a child, if you suffered bullying and rejection from people around you, you might have grown up thinking you are not good enough, and that is why you got picked on. If not checked, you might grow up with this mindset and you will start avoiding people in general. Other extreme experiences such as rape and parental conflicts, can also increase a child's chances of having SAD.

One's Personality: Some people are naturally withdrawn and shy. These people are more prone to social anxiety disorder when compared with their bold and daring counterparts.

A demanding ordeal might also trigger it: For instance, if your dream is to be a performer, and on your first day of mounting the stage, you performed very badly and got booed off stage, you might dread having that experience again, and withdraw yourself from public appearance.

Having a feature that attracts attention: This is one of the most common causes of social anxiety. Common examples are facial disfigurement, speech impediments such as stuttering, and health conditions such as Parkinson's disease. Features like these may keep them on edge, and so they have a higher level of self-consciousness. This heightened self-consciousness can culminate into social anxiety, especially if the bearer gets insulted for such a feature.

As you have seen in this discourse, there is no particular single cause for SAD. What we have are a bunch of factors that could combine to cause it. When we start looking at the solutions later in this book, we will look at why it is important to find out the root cause of SAD during treatment.

What Are the Physical Symptoms?

People with SAD are too conscious of other people's assessments of them, and oftentimes, they believe the assessment is negative. The following physical symptoms will often manifest. For example, if you are giving a speech and you stutter just once, you might think that everyone in the room picked it up on it, but it's far more likely that they didn't. You will then tell yourself that you are a terrible public speaker, and these people know it. This thought pattern will make you stutter more, sweat, or tremble.

The common physical symptoms are:

- Blushing
- Difficulty talking

- Stammering
- Shaking or trembling
- Increased heart rate
- Fast pace of breathing
- Sweating
- Mind going blank
- Lightheadedness
- Difficulty concentrating
- Urge to use the toilet
- Dizziness
- Muscle tension
- Vomiting
- Nausea or stomach upset
- Urge to escape or leave
- Stumbling and falling when walking past a group of people. This happens when you become worried about the way you walk.
- Crying
- Dry mouth and throat
- Clammy and cold hands
- Diarrhea
- Heart palpitations
- Feelings of unreality (derealization)
- Feelings of detachment from oneself (depersonalization)
- Paresthesias (tingling)
- Red face
- Hot flashes
- Shortness of breath

What Are the Behavioral Symptoms?

In terms of behavior, a person with social anxiety has gone beyond shyness, and also has convinced himself that he is no good. To avoid being embarrassed for his perceived flaws, he chooses to avoid situations altogether.

The common behavioral symptoms are:

- Avoiding the situation altogether
- Avoiding similar sorts of situations
- Leaving prematurely
- Focusing on yourself
- Trying not to draw attention to yourself
- Keeping quiet
- Not looking at other people

What are the emotional symptoms?

The dominant emotional symptoms of those with social anxiety are:

- Anxiety and nervousness
- High levels of inexplicable fear
- Automatic negative emotional cycles
- In some severe but rare cases, people can even develop dysmorphia for any part of their body (mostly the face), and they will start considering themselves irrationally and negatively.

Out of all the emotional symptoms stated above, incessant and intense anxiety (fear) is the most prevalent one.

Some Negative Beliefs and Maladaptive Behavior That Can Increase Social Anxiety

People with social anxiety have some negative beliefs. These negative beliefs are more pronounced whenever there is an upcoming social situation or event. To them, these thoughts are meant to protect them from the various threats they perceive. Psychologists, Asta Klimaite, John Clarke, and Kathryn Smerling, reported some of these thoughts patterns as stated below:

"I am probably going to embarrass myself."

"I might not blend in with the rest."

"Nobody will like me."

"The people there will hate me."

"I might even pass out."

"My nervousness will show, and people will notice."

"I will not be able to say anything because I won't know what to say."

"I am not going to offer anything."

"People will not like to befriend me."

"I might even say something stupid."

"I have problems."

Something all of the statements above have in common is that they all have to do with low self-esteem. These statements are born of an inner lack of confidence. When you feel like you are unworthy, you will likely also feel you don't have anything to offer. You will then tell yourself that since you don't have anything to offer, you are not likable and that means you don't deserve social interaction like everyone else.

To be sure that the statements above don't play out as prophesied, a person in this situation will choose to bypass the social gathering. When they do this, it has immediate benefits because it allows them to escape the symptoms they dread so much. But what about the long-term demerits? The demerits of not living your life to the fullest and limiting yourself.

In this chapter, you have learned why people get anxious in social situations, the different causes of the anxious feeling, and the symptoms of anxiety (both physical and behavioral). In the next chapter, I will be giving you tips on how to deal with SAD. The tips are to help you cope and live a better life.

CHAPTER THREE:

Tips for Dealing with Social Anxiety

By this point, you should have a good idea if you have social anxiety. Feeling too anxious and inhibited when meeting people, speaking in front of people, using public restrooms or locker rooms, and eating in public are some of the common signs of social anxiety.

A lot of people with this issue will choose to ignore the signs and avoid social situations instead of facing the facts and seeking help. Like I mentioned earlier, they may even choose to use drugs and alcohol to self-medicate. However, self-medicating isn't the way out, as it can lead to an increased risk for depression, alcohol abuse, and loneliness.

To an extent, social anxiety affects a lot of people, and the good news here is that something can be done about it. In this chapter, I will be giving you some tips on how to cope with anxiety and make your life easier, happier, and more fulfilling. Let's take a look at some of those helpful tips:

Learn to Face Your Fears

As humans, it is very natural to avoid scary emotions. No one would want to walk into what already seems like a painful experience blindly. Usually, this is about you hiding from possible challenges that contribute to your joy and overall growth. You can't always hide away from this fear; it will still strike back no matter how hard you try to suppress it. It is even more likely to strike back when you need emotional equanimity the most.

If you learn how to face your fears, you will have better control of your decisions and your life. One effective way to learn how to face your fears is by facing the social situations which you are always scared of. A lot of people with social anxiety will rather avoid situations, but avoidance will only keep fueling your social anxiety.

Of course, avoiding some nerve-wracking situations can make you feel better, but it's all in the short-term. In the long run, it will prevent you from being comfortable in social situations, and you still won't know how to cope with it. For a fact, the more you keep avoiding your fears, the more those fears become frightening.

Avoiding your fears can also stop you from reaching goals you've set for yourself, and prevent you from doing the things you love to do. For example, because you are scared to speak in a group, you'd rather hide your great ideas. Because you are scared of making new friends, you'd rather be quiet and lose people who would've helped you get out of a particular situation. There are so many examples where your fear will make you lose what you should have gained.

Though it may seem somehow impossible to overcome your fear of social situations, there is still hope, and you can take it one step at a time. What you need to do is to start with situations that you can manage, and slowly work your way up to the more challenging ones. In no time, you will gain some coping skills and boost your confidence as you gradually move through the anxiety ladder.

Let's take socializing with people as an example. If it makes you feel very anxious, a way to gradually face your fears is to attend a party with a close friend – someone you are already very accustomed to. At the very least, you won't be alone or feel uncomfortable since you have a close friend around. If you continue this way, you will eventually get comfortable with this step, and then you can proceed and try introducing yourself to a stranger you meet at the party.

Another way people avoid their fears is by always being on social media or burying their nose in their phone. We live in a smart world where everything (and everyone) is always connected. So, when we experience fear of social situations, we can easily utilize our smartphones by hiding behind the phone to chat with people, know what is going on in people's lives without asking them face-to-face, and make new friends online, just to avoid social interactions. This can only do you more harm than good despite giving short-term satisfaction.

According to a 2016 study of young adults and smartphones, there were "significant positive correlations" between the overuse of smartphones and an occurrence of social anxiety.

Another 2017 study revealed that out of the 182 young adults who were smartphone users, people that showed addiction to technology displayed social anxiety, low self-esteem, and isolation.

The evolution of the world has made smartphones give us a sense of connection. According to Isaac Vaghefi, an assistant professor of management information systems at Binghamton University, New York, smartphones are a tool that gives us that immediate, short, and quick satisfaction, and it can be very triggering.

In the end, you will realize that hiding behind your smartphone can only delay you in addressing your fear of social situations. At first, you will see that facing your fears is actually scarier and can be counterintuitive, but it is always better to face your fears through a gradual process.

According to researchers, a crucial approach in the treatment of fear that stems from social anxiety is an intentional exposure to social mishaps. The goal here is to disrupt the person's supposed standards and social norms deliberately, just to break the cycle of further use of avoidance strategies and fearful anticipations.

As a result of this, people are compelled to reassess the perceived threat of a social situation after realizing that the social mishaps don't usually lead to the feared irreparable, long-lasting, and undesirable consequences. To put it simply, by intentionally approaching social situations, you will learn that a small number of slips shouldn't lead to exclusions and rejection by social groups. We are all human, and make mistakes on occasions, too; no one is above making mistakes.

For you to effectively work your way right up a society anxiety ladder, try out the tips below:

- Take it one step at a time, and don't face your biggest fear immediately. Moving too fast in climbing the ladder is never a good idea, as you may feel too embarrassed and decide to hide yourself more. Instead, take it slow, don't force things, and don't take too much since it is a gradual process.
- Exercise patience. To fully overcome social anxiety, you will need to be patient because it takes enough practice and time to master your emotions. You shouldn't give up after one or two tries and say you have done your best, the results may not be visible at that time, but will definitely be seen later.
- Learn to stay calm with the skills you have learned. You can stay calm by focusing on your breathing, taking in deep breaths, and challenging any form of negative norms.

Keep Away Negative Coping Strategies

Some psychological symptoms come from the negative mental and emotional states linked with social anxiety. This can worsen your social anxiety and makes you feel more isolated. Sometimes, you may find it so tempting to take drugs or drink alcohol to help you feel at ease and comfortable, but to be honest, these can only increase your level of anxiety.

Research revealed that social anxiety isn't limited to just inner feelings like shakiness in one's voice or having a brain fog that hinders one from thinking straight, but also has physical feelings like a loss of appetite, stomach upset, muscle stiffness, sweaty hands, and feeling faint. When people like this find themselves in social situations they can't avoid, probably a school event where a lot of people will be in attendance, they try to dampen the symptoms of their social anxiety by using some negative coping strategies. For example, smoking cigarettes or drinking alcohol.

While you may feel good after a few puffs and maybe even less worried, smoking too much will most likely make the anxiety get worse. The same thing with drinking alcohol, drinking too much of it will increase your level of anxiety. Too much alcohol intake could cause a bad mood, increased level of anxiety, and disrupted sleep patterns.

The Anxiety and Depression Association of America (ADAA) reported that about 20% of people that have social anxiety also have an alcohol use disorder. It was also revealed that the findings are associated with adults and adolescents struggling with social anxiety.

A very helpful tip that can keep your anxiety in check and help stay clear of the potential chance to worsen your anxiety symptoms is to avoid any negative strategy you have set aside to help you get by. Avoid drinking alcohol, no matter how promising the initial relaxation it gives you. It might feel comforting, but will definitely hurt you in the long run.

On the other hand, leading a healthy lifestyle, eating well, exercising regularly, and avoiding alcohol can help you cope with social anxiety.

Change your Perspective

Changing your perspective is another great tip that will help you deal with your social anxiety. By changing your understanding of the stress you are going through, you will be able to deal with anxiety better.

The major problem I see in people with SAD is that they see all stress as bad and damaging. They dread being in social situations and the thought of it alone triggers stress. If only they get to change their perspectives, and look at things from a different point of view, they wouldn't see stress as damaging. In 2013, Jeremy Jamieson, an assistant professor of psychology at the University of Rochester, New York, conducted a study with his colleagues. In the study, it was realized that when an individual suffers from social anxiety or not, and knows how his or her body reacts to some stressors (e.g., public speaking), he will experience a little stress even in uncomfortable social situations. Meaning, they won't need to feel stressed from the social situation.

When we hear of "killer stress," our mind races, and we picture being stressed out. What it means is that our body is just preparing itself to tackle a demanding situation. It is putting together the necessary resources, delivering oxygen to the brain, and pumping blood to the major muscle groups. When we understand that there shouldn't be a cause for alarm, we will feel more at ease. Research has suggested that a coping tool that helps with negative thoughts and worries is by embracing the "yes, but" technique. This technique is all about you challenging your negative thoughts and offset them with a positive one.

For example, if you are thinking about a social situation and beginning to experience anxiety, say: "Yes, I will be attending a social gathering today where many people will be in attendance," and go ahead and add… "But, I am also an amazing person with great attributes; there will be so much to talk about when I meet people."

To switch things up for negative thoughts, one needs to counter his or her fear with positive thoughts and likely positive affirmation. This will help you reaffirm yourself and know you are making the right decision. Like I said earlier, dealing with social anxiety comes with you facing your fear, and having positive affirmations helps you do this.

Be Confident

Confidence is so magical that when you have it in abundance, it will open doors for you. It is one priceless thing that a lot of people wouldn't mind spending money for – yet it is something we all can develop. A lot of adults are crippled by shyness and social phobias; they lack the confidence to face people or be heard and seen.

Confidence is something that can be learned, just the way you would learn to ride a bike or acquire a skill: you get better at it with lots of practice. Try to act more confidently in your appearance, the way you talk, and the way you act, and you will see how positively people will react. I am not saying you should ridicule yourself, be a clown, or make a spectacle of yourself just to be seen as confident. What I mean is being more firm in whatever you do. At first, it will definitely feel terrifying, and you might want to take a step back; but you shouldn't because it only gets better each time. Practice makes perfect!

Gaining confidence doesn't happen overnight; it requires conscious effort from you just the way developing other skills require effort. By avoiding social interactions, your social anxiety will still be as it is, but when you choose to face your fears and stop avoiding them, you become ready to fight your social anxiety.

Do Something Nice for Someone

Doing something nice for someone is one good way of being in control of social situations and helps distract you from any concerns or negative thoughts you have. When I say doing something nice, you don't need to buy an extravagant gift or do more than you can afford, but a simple act of kindness will do the trick for counteracting your social anxiety.

Research has suggested that being kind can have a positive effect on one's mood. A 2017 study revealed that doing something nice for someone will activate the area in the brain that is linked to motivation and the reward cycle (Cohut, 2017).

Another 2015 study that was published in the journal *Motivation and Emotion* suggested that acting selflessly can help people with social anxiety feel more at ease when in social situations. In that same study, people who were actively involved in showing kindness to each other later on felt the need to be less avoidant of social situations. The act of kindness can be helping a stranger cross the street or helping a neighbor mow his lawn (Trew & Alden, 2015).

According to Jennifer Trew, who is one of the study authors from Simon Fraser University in Burnaby, Canada, being kind is something that will help you counter those negative social expectations by encouraging the positive expectations and perceptions of one's social environment. Kindness can reduce the level of your social anxiety and make you feel less likely to stay away from social situations.

A report from Medical News Today (MNT) published in August 2019 showed the importance of replacing negative links with positive ones in order to reduce social anxiety. For instance, by replacing bad experiences with good ones. In a bid to do this, some people were interviewed, and someone had this to say:

"People have a negative narrative in their head because that narrative comes from memories of awkward or embarrassing moments that override everything else, so if you one good interaction, you can use that momentum in the same way to get yourself another, and another. Before you know it, you have a library of positive references, and you naturally find that negative self-talk diminishing."

In the end, it all boils down to having a better mental environment.

Take a Breath

A lot of changes take place when your body is experiencing anxiety. Some of the physical symptoms linked to anxiety are dizziness, pounding chest, increased heart rate, and muscle tension. By taking a minute to slow down, your breath can position you better and be in control of your body. When it comes to breathing techniques, there are several of them that are effective in helping you calm and relax your body. I will be focusing more on the diaphragmatic breathing as a relaxation technique, later in this book.

For now, we are focusing on how to take a breath. You can start by taking a seat, be comfortable, and try to take the biggest breath you have ever taken for that day and hold it. Count from 1 to 4, then exhale slowly and push out as much air as possible. Again, take another deep breath by filling your stomach with air, and continue doing so until you realize that your breath is beginning to slow down to its normal rate.

Finally, to deal with social anxiety effectively, you need to identify those situations you avoid. Start by making a list of these types of situations, or situations that make you feel anxious just thinking about, for example, eating outside. You are in fear that people might observe how you eat or ease yourself and decide to avoid such situations — same thing with speaking in front of a group or saying hello to a stranger.

So, ask yourself, what situations provoke your anxiety, and what do you avoid? Make a list of them and know what you are dealing with. In the next chapter, I will be going deeper by showing you ways in which you can overcome anxiety.

In this chapter, I provided some useful tips you can use to deal with SAD. Using the tips requires us to make some changes in our lives. In the next chapter, I will be explaining what it means to overcome anxiety and the different ways to do so.

CHAPTER FOUR:

Overcoming Social Anxiety

Your palms are sweaty, your mind is racing, and you are finding it so difficult to bring words out of your mouth, no matter how hard you try… we've all experienced this feeling at one time or another, but some of us experience it worse, and more often than others – it all points to social anxiety.

No one wants to be embarrassed or look stupid around people, but the extreme end of this spectrum of thinking causes people to avoid social situations just to be "socially safe." But, have you asked yourself why you keep avoiding social situations so much? Your life isn't on the line, and you won't be losing anything. Yet, you keep avoiding it.

I can easily recall the same discomfort you feel when you're in public. Conversely, it can be difficult to remember physical pain with the same detail, for example, when you hit your leg on the table so badly a few days ago. So it's no surprise that research revealed humans feel social pain much more than they feel physical pain, and social pain can be relived over and over again.

In a paper by the German Socio-Economic Panel Study (SOEP) titled "Perceived Job Insecurity and Well-Being Revisited: Towards Conceptual Clarity," it was revealed that the fear associated with losing one's job is more painful than when the job is actually lost.

Most of the advice we get on how to overcome social anxiety is usually a dead end. We may have been told to just "suppress the feelings" when it comes. But what happens when the feelings are suppressed? Our ability to experience positive feelings is on the low but not the negative feelings. So what do we do then the negative feelings start creeping out?

I've rounded up some of the best strategies, from ancient stoics, mindfulness experts, and neuroscientists, to help people deal with their negative feelings associated with their anxiety disorder. The good news is that it's not that hard to do. You only need to study it, practice it, and get better at it. Now, let's move on to how you can overcome your social anxiety:

Challenge Your Negative Thoughts

Sometimes, finding relief or getting a lasting solution for social anxiety may seem impossible, but there are a lot of things that can help you. First, you need to challenge your negative thoughts. If you have social anxiety, then you should be familiar with some negative beliefs and thoughts which normally give birth to your fear and anxiety. Some of these negative thoughts can be:

- "I might make a mess of myself."
- "I don't want to be seen as a fool."
- "I might be at a loss for words and won't know what to say."
- "My hands might start trembling, and I'll end up embarrassing myself."

If you go with these negative thoughts by choosing to avoid the situation, you can only experience short-term relief, but you keep allowing the social anxiety to own you. But when you choose to challenge these thoughts, you are fighting to gain back control of your life, and your symptoms of anxiety will spiral down in no time.

To effectively challenge your negative thoughts, follow the tips below:

- Identify the negative thoughts that fuel your anxiety. For instance, if you are in a class and you are so scared that you will get called upon by your teacher to answer a question, the underlying negative thought can be "If I get called upon, I am going to embarrass myself and everyone will laugh at me."

- Evaluate and challenge negative thoughts. You can start by asking yourself questions. Questions like, "Why do I think I will embarrass myself?" or "Even if I fail to answer the question, am I not in the school to learn?" By logically evaluating your negative thoughts, you can now replace the thoughts with more positive and realistic ways you view social situations, which usually trigger your anxiety.

Thinking about why you think and feel the way you do can be terrifying at first, but at least when you understand the reasons that fuel your fear and anxiety, you can decrease the chances of it interrupting your life.

There are some unhelpful thinking styles you might be inculcating in yourself. It won't do you any good, but it will fuel your anxiety. Below are some of the unhelpful thinking styles. Take a look at them, and honestly determine if you are engaging in any of them. If you are, now is a good time to call it quits.

- Personalizing. This is when you assume people focus on you in a negative way, or what happens with others concerns you.
- Mind reading. You assume people know what you are thinking, and they see you the same way you see yourself (negative).
- Catastrophizing. By blowing things beyond proportion. You think it is a terrible thing for people to see you nervous.
- Fortune telling. You start predicting the future by assuming the worst will happen to you, or things will go horribly. This will only create anxiety within you.

Focus Less on Yourself and More on Others

It is quite difficult to put a stop to the countless thoughts that run through your mind when you are in situations that make you particularly anxious. When dealing with social anxiety, it is easier to turn inward and focus on yourself and how others see you, always thinking it will definitely be negative. Just like that familiar thought of people looking at you when you get called upon to answer a question in class. But that isn't always the case. You need to stop focusing on yourself and what others think about you. Instead, focus on people, be mindful, and work to form true bonds.

It's easy to get caught up in anxious feelings and thoughts when in social situations that make you nervous. You are already convinced that all eyes are on you, and judging you, while you focus on your bodily sensations. You might think that when you pay more attention to how your body reacts, you will have better control of it.

On the downside, the extra focus you are giving yourself only increases your awareness of your nervous feeling, and this triggers more anxiety. It also stops you from giving full concentration to the conversations around you and how you perform.

When you switch to an external focus rather than an internal focus, it will make a difference in reducing your social anxiety. As I'm sure you'll agree, trying to pay full attention to two things at once can be very distracting. A better approach is to focus on the things happening around you, than trying to toggle between focusing on two things at once.

Adapt to the mentality that people are not thinking negative things about you, even if they notice you are a bit nervous. Humans are not perfect, so free yourself, be in the moment, and listen to what the other person is saying.

In a study, three candidates were assessed for the same job. In the end, the interviewee that spilled coffee on his shirt but scored high was chosen. The ideal candidate that made little to no mistake was not given the job. The reason the hiring manager gave was that the ideal candidate wasn't enviable as he was looking too perfect. (Barker, 2018).

The study suggested that being too perfect can have its repercussions. So, why not just be yourself and allow people to accept you for who you are?

Another research study showed that when people meet someone for the first time, they evaluate the meeting by looking at how well they perform instead of focusing on the topic of discussion. Try to be a good listener and be attentive to what the other person is saying; these are traits that are welcomed in conversations.

If this sounds like something that doesn't come naturally to you, just follow the tips below to learn how to focus on others more easily:

- Focus your attention on others, but not what they think of you. Try to engage them and make a true connection.
- Always remember anxiety isn't that visible. If someone notices that you are nervous, you shouldn't conclude that they think badly of you. There is a high chance that the other person is also nervous, just like you, or have also been nervous in the past before overcoming it.
- Listen more to what is actually being said, and less about your negative thoughts. The negative thoughts will only feed your anxiety.
- Be in the present. Try to focus on the present moment rather than worrying too much about what you will say next, or beating yourself up for a stumble that's already in the past.
- Don't be pressured to be perfect. Rather, try to be your true self, and be observant of the qualities people value.

Be More Social

Another way of challenging your fears and overcoming anxiety is to seek out supportive social environments. Instead of staying cooped up indoors, try to get out of your house (and your shell) and relate more with people. You can try out the suggestions below:

- Enroll in an assertiveness training class or social skills class. Classes like these are usually offered at community colleges or local adult education centers. So check around to know which is accessible to you.
- Volunteer. Being a volunteer can be enjoyable if you choose what you are comfortable with. You can choose to stuff

envelopes for campaigns, or clean up around your community. Just do anything that you can focus on while also meeting new people.
- Develop your communication skills. Forming good relationships is influenced by the emotional intelligence skill of communication. If it is difficult for you to connect with people, then you should learn the basic skills of emotional intelligence.

Adapt to An Anti-Anxiety Lifestyle

Your body and mind are naturally linked. Research suggests that the way you treat your body has an effect on your anxiety level and how you manage your anxiety symptoms. Even though adopting lifestyle changes alone aren't enough to overcome your fears, it can support the other tips and treatment of anxiety disorder. Let's take a look at some lifestyle tips that will help you keep your anxiety symptoms at bay and support you in overcoming your anxiety.

- Be active. You need to prioritize taking part in physical activity. You can start by setting aside thirty minutes of your time daily to exercise. If you are not a fan of exercise, you can pair it with an activity you enjoy. For example, dancing to your favorite tunes, or consider running to the bus stop every day.
- Limit or avoid your caffeine intake. Tea, coffee, energy drinks, and soda all act as stimulants that can increase your anxiety symptoms. You should consider limiting your caffeine intake to just mornings, or cut it off totally.
- Introduce more omega-3 fats to your diet. The roles of omega-3 fatty acids are to support your brain health, improve your outlook, mood, and strengthen your ability to handle anxiety symptoms. To get omega-3 fatty acids, you should consider consuming fatty fish like herring, salmon, sardines, anchovies, and mackerel. Other foods are walnuts, flaxseed, and seaweed.
- Quit smoking. Cigarettes contain nicotine, which is a powerful stimulant. Some people smoke to make them feel better, however, smoking will only increase your anxiety level, not

decrease it. If you are addicted, you need to curb the habit to feel better.
- Drink alcohol moderately. When in a social situation, you may be tempted to drink alcohol, hoping it will calm down your nerves. Too much alcohol will only increase your risk of having an anxiety attack.
- Get quality sleep. Being sleep deprived will only make you defenseless to anxiety. Try to get enough quality sleep to help you remain calm when in stressful situations.

Create Objective Goals

When you feel anxious, you usually don't care to see the positives. Who knows? You might actually do great in the situation, but the anxiety wouldn't let you know, you choose to see your performance as awful. For this reason, therapists urge patients to create objective behavioral goals. These behavioral goals are what people around you will see and observe. How you feel (fear) or what you do (sweating, trembling, or blushing) doesn't matter, especially since you don't have control of them when in a social situation.

So, when you are working in a team, your objective behavior should be to voice your opinion. This will help you measure your progress. Also, you won't be focusing on yourself and whether you are nervous. Instead, you will be focusing on whether you achieved your goal.

You should also avoid focusing on people's reactions. How your teammates received your idea at the meeting shouldn't bother you because what matters most is that you took that first bold step to speak up. It doesn't matter if someone turned down your request; at least you asked. It doesn't matter if you can't always agree with someone else's opinion; your opinion matters, too. After all, you did what was needed, and you can't control people's actions.

Be Mindful

Practicing mindfulness meditation and being present in your environment and thoughts will make you be aware of your feelings and thoughts in a more positive and non-judgmental way.

According to a study published in the journal Social Cognitive and Affective Neuroscience, researchers revealed the impact meditation has on activities, specifically in the areas of the brain. The participants with a normal level of anxiety had taken part in four twenty-minute mindfulness meditation classes. It was discovered that there was a 39% decrease in anxiety levels of participants after partaking in mindfulness training.

Several other studies have revealed the benefits of mindfulness meditation to the body – it doesn't just reduce anxiety level but that of depression too. Research from the University of Amsterdam suggested that mindfulness training is a more accessible, cost-effective, and effective way to treat a social anxiety disorder (Bögels, 2014).

During mindfulness training, patients will be taught how to be in more control of their attention and reinforce their ability to be present by using meditation techniques.

Create An Exposure Hierarchy Social Anxiety

The exposure hierarchy is a list (similar to a ladder), where you chronologically write down the situations that trigger your anxiety, according to how serious it is. After writing them down, you perform the easiest of the behaviors, and keep going until you have completed all those you have listed.

You can start by identifying and rating how anxious each social situation makes you feel. For instance, the number "0" stands for no anxiety, while "10" would be the highest anxiety you have ever felt. Now, make a list of how you would feel in any situation, no matter how big or small it is — ranging from asking a stranger for help or presenting in front of a class. Also, write down your predictions, so that it won't be new to you when it's time to experience it.

Start testing your predictions, record your social situations, and how you felt. After a series of records, you may find out that talking to a stranger is now a "4" instead of the "9" you first predicted. This tracking helps you keep a record and track your progress, which is usually encouraging.

Learn to Talk

Hopefully, when trying to overcome shyness and social anxiety, you will learn how to be more confident when talking to people. I know how challenging talking to other people can be, even thinking of what to say can trigger anxiety. An awkward silence can feel like a lifetime, and it can be embarrassing, not knowing what to say next. However, you can start small by gradually talking to people, and this will help you feel less anxious each time you try.

You can apply some conversational techniques to help you get started. Ask open-ended questions and let the other person do most of the talking. Ask questions that don't require just a yes or no answer, ask personal questions with the hope of taking the conversation to a deeper level. Doing this will help you get to know the other person more. Once you start feeling comfortable and confident, you can now share some of your personal information. This is like an invitation for the person to ask you deeper questions, too.

Be Kind to Yourself

As humans, we are not perfect, and everyone is bound to make a mistake and feel humiliated at some point. What I want you to know is that overcoming anxiety is not that easy and not something you can do in one day; so cut yourself some slack!

There are times you will start thinking negatively, start losing your grip, and maybe even slip back into your bad habits. If you are feeling tired or stressed, you may start feeling more anxious, but never think that you have simply failed. All you need to do is take a minute and be kind to yourself. You will need patience and self-compassion to succeed, and they are your keys to freedom. If you are having a bad day, don't give up. Just be kind to yourself and get back up.

The Anxiety and Depression Association of America (ADAA), estimated that one-third of people suffering from social anxiety disorder procrastinated and waited for about ten years before speaking to a professional. This anxiety disorder has negative effects on many different aspects of life – ranging from your personal relationships to your workplace relationships.

I have given you some great ways to help you overcome your social anxiety. Even if it looks like a daunting task, it's worth trying so that you can live your best life. No matter how nervous you feel when in social situations, learn to silence your self-critical thoughts and be more confident in interacting with others. By learning and going over what I have given you above, you will learn to overcome your fears and build great and rewarding relationships.

Overcoming social anxiety is a gradual process that requires time for the new neural route for social interactions to be created. If your social anxiety doesn't get better and keeps interfering with your daily life after following all the tips I have given, then don't hesitate to seek professional help.

After having an idea of how to overcome anxiety, what's next? In the next chapter, I will be explaining some relaxation techniques you can use, how they work, and how to practice them.

CHAPTER FIVE:

Relaxation Techniques

In an everyday context, what do we mean when we say we are relaxed? Most of the time, when we say we are relaxed, we are simply saying that we are free from tension. Bringing it back to social anxiety, we see why it is important. If social anxiety makes you tense, then relaxation techniques should be able to help rid you of that tension.

Relaxation is closely related to mindfulness and meditation, but it is different. Consider relaxation as the end, while mindfulness and meditation are the means of getting there. For instance, when you do yoga or other mental exercises, you control your breath and your thoughts until you bring your whole body into a relaxed mode. What you just did is using mindfulness to achieve relaxation. So it stands to reason that certain conditions, like anxiety, that can destabilize the calmness of the body can be managed through certain relaxation techniques.

Several relaxation techniques have proven to be very effective against anxiety disorders, including social anxiety. These relaxation techniques are combined with other treatments for better results, especially in very severe cases. But it can also be used alone to counter many of the symptoms of social anxiety. For instance, relaxation techniques such as deep breathing and muscle relaxation can calm the nerves during a speech.

Is There Proof That It Works?

Several studies have been conducted to know if relaxation techniques are effective against social anxiety. One such study is a meta-analysis of fifty studies covering 2,801 patients. This study compared the results obtained from treating patients using relaxation techniques and those obtained with cognitive and behavioral treatments (CBT). The researchers found that there was no marked difference between the results. Don't forget that CBT is supposed to be the main psychological treatment for social anxiety. So if relaxation techniques perform just as well, then they too are effective against social anxiety.

Another meta-analysis study that was conducted in 2018 showed that relaxation techniques, when used for people with social anxiety, helped them reduce negative emotions such as depression, worry, and phobia.

Now that we have proof that it works, let us now look at some of the relaxation techniques you can use.

Relaxation Techniques for Social Anxiety

Diaphragmatic Breathing

Diaphragmatic breathing, also known as deep breathing, is a breathing pattern in which you expand your diaphragm so that your chest doesn't rise and fall, rather it is your stomach that does that. By doing this, you are taking deeper breaths and helping to alleviate your symptoms. Breathing is very important to life as it helps in supplying your body and organs with oxygen that is vital for survival. So, when you don't breathe well, it will upset the exchange of oxygen and carbon dioxide, which can contribute to anxiety.

Ideally, you don't have to wait until you have an anxiety attack before trying to pull up diaphragmatic breathing. Rather, you are expected to keep practicing it even when you are relaxed so that when it is time to use it, it will come to you easily. Otherwise, you might find it difficult to perform when the anxiety is already upon you. Another reason why you must practice deep breathing is that other relaxation techniques are based on it, making it an important technique to master.

How Important is Diaphragmatic Breathing?

When you are tense, your body enters what we call "fight-or-flight" mode. In this mode, your body is at alert, pretty much like when you are in a fight. If you are fighting, for instance, your body goes into this mode because it wants you to see and avoid as many physical attacks as possible. Most of your body processes are racing at such a time. To balance this increase, your heart beats faster to circulate enough blood. This can be normal if you are a normal person, and you are in an emergency. But if you are a person with social anxiety and you are in what you erroneously believe to be an emergency, this situation can quickly degenerate into an anxiety attack.

What deep breathing does for you, in this case, is that it helps you become aware of the changes in your body and helps you slow down the heart rate by dictating the pace and depth. This way, your body begins to realize there was no emergency, after all, just a harmless social situation. With this, your likelihood of escalating into an anxiety attack is greatly reduced.

How Can I Practice Diaphragmatic Breathing?

I mentioned before that it is good to get your body used to this pattern of breathing so that you can easily do it when the need arises. Now let me show you how you can practice diaphragmatic breathing, even when you are alone and already relaxed.

See the steps you can take to practice deep breathing:

1. Find a place that is free of distraction. When you are initially starting, you don't want any form of distraction, so that you can focus on your breath. That is why a quiet place, free of distractions, is vital. You also need to find a position that allows you enough relaxation, such as lying face up or reclining in a

chair. Relax all your muscles. You also need to feel free, so items such as glasses, a watch, or tight clothing may not be ideal.
2. To ensure that you are breathing correctly, make sure it is your stomach that rises and drops when you breathe in and breathe out, you need to place one hand on your chest, the other on your stomach, and ensure that the one your chest doesn't move during the exercise. With your hands in place, take a deep breath from your abdomen and count a slow one, two, three, to ensure the breath was really deep enough.
3. Pause the breath for a short while and exhale slowly while repeating your one, two, three count. Ensure it is your stomach that is falling back and not your chest.
4. Repeat the exercise for five to ten minutes, until your body is relaxed.

Continue doing this for several days until you master it. If you are having issues mastering the technique, you can join a yoga class or mindfulness meditation class. These classes will teach you some other techniques that also use deep breathing so that you can go past the task of mastering deep breathing.

Autogenic Training

Ever heard the saying "there is power in the word"? You must have, and it seems to be true that it is the very foundation of autogenic training. In this training, you are repeatedly telling yourself things that can get you relaxed. In autogenic training, you are telling yourself things like, "I am relaxed now." It is thought that when you repeat these statements to yourself, you can influence the way your autonomic nervous system functions. And it is the autonomic nervous system that controls heart rate.

A 2008 meta-analysis study by Stretter F. and Kupper S. showed that the autogenic technique is indeed effective for treating anxiety. If it can treat anxiety, then you can also use it to calm yourself down whenever you find yourself in a social situation.

So How Can You Practice It?

When preparing for autogenic exercise, the steps are similar to those for diaphragmatic breathing. Ensure you get to a place that is free of distractions, and ensure that you also feel free by avoiding tight or distracting clothing. Ensure you are lying flat on the floor, or you are reclining in a chair.

For the actual exercise, do the following:

- Start by practicing diaphragmatic breathing for a couple of minutes. Then gently tell yourself the words, "I am calm."
- Next, focus your attention on your arms. Then tell yourself, "My arms are heavy." Repeat it six more times. Then calmly tell yourself, "I am calm."
- Focus your attention on your arms again. This time quietly tell yourself, "My arms are warm." Repeat six more times. Then calmly tell yourself, "I am calm."
- Shift your attention to your legs and quietly tell yourself, "My legs are heavy." Repeat six more times. Then calmly tell yourself, "I am calm."
- Pay attention to your legs again. Do the same thing by calmly telling yourself, "My legs are very warm." Do this six more times. Then calmly tell yourself, "I am calm."
- Move on to your heartbeat. Focus your attention on it and calmly repeat to yourself, "My heart is beating calmly and regularly." Then calmly tell yourself, "I am calm."
- Next, you focus on your breath. Tell yourself calmly, "My breathing is calm and regular." Then calmly tell yourself, "I am calm."
- Focus your attention on your abdomen and quietly tell yourself, "My abdomen is warm." Do this six more times, then calmly tell yourself, "I am calm."
- Next is your forehead, quietly repeat to yourself, "My forehead is pleasantly cool." Do this six more times, then calmly tell yourself, "I am calm."

- Notice your body relaxing and enjoy the feeling that comes with it. Then calmly and quietly tell yourself, "My arms are firm, I breathe deeply, and my eyes are open."

Progressive muscle relaxation

People who suffer from social anxiety disorder experience tensed muscles a lot. This muscle tension is coming from the fact that they are on edge. That is why progressive muscle relaxation (PMR) is very effective for people with social and anxiety. PMR is an anxiety-reduction technique that seeks to eliminate tension from the major muscle groups and to replace them with relaxation. It was first introduced in 1930 by the American physician Edmund Jacobson.

This technique is so effective against anxiety and tension that if done properly, it can even make you fall asleep. If you master it, you will be amazed by the difference between a tensed muscle and a relaxed muscle. The latter is priceless. You should look forward to achieving it.

Just as other relaxation techniques, it can be used by itself or combined with others for a stronger effect. Also, it requires practice to acclimatize you with it. So practice it even when you are relaxed, so that when you are not, you can easily get your mind to do it.

Below are the steps for practicing Progressive Muscle Relaxation (PMR)

Like others before it, start by finding a quiet place, free of distractions. Begin in a very relaxed posture, such as lying flat or reclining on a chair. Try to stay away from tight or distracting clothing, and remove items that might bother you, such as earphones, glasses, watches, or bracelets. When you are ready, use the first six to seven minutes to practice your deep breathing.

After that, do the following, while keeping your body relaxed.

- Start with your forehead. Squeeze the muscles in your forehead gently and hold for about fifteen seconds. You will feel the muscles becoming tense. Then gently release while counting

down for thirty seconds. You should notice the sensation of relaxation that overtakes the muscles. For best results, do this while breathing slowly and evenly.
- Next, move to your jaw. As with the forehead, tense the muscles in your jaw for about fifteen seconds and start to release the tension while counting down from thirty. While doing this, try to pay attention to the relaxation that comes to that region. Also, make sure that you are breathing slowly and deeply.
- Move on to your neck and shoulders. Apply tension to the muscles in this region by raising your shoulders and holding in place for about fifteen seconds. Then gently release the tension while counting down from thirty.
- Gently draw your hands into fists. Pull your formed fists towards your chest and hold in place for fifteen seconds. Squeeze the fists tightly and hold them very close to your chest. As with the previous exercises, release while counting down from thirty, and notice the relaxation that follows.
- Then move on to your buttocks. Simply increase the tension in your buttocks and hold for fifteen seconds. After the fifteen seconds, gradually release the tension while counting down from thirty. Breathe slowly and notice relaxation replacing the tension.
- For the legs, target your calves and quadriceps. Calmly squeeze and hold them for fifteen seconds, then release gradually for a time interval of thirty seconds.
- Lastly, slowly and calmly increase the tension in both your feet and toes, as much as you can. Release while counting down from thirty. Breathe slowly and notice the tension disappearing.

With this last one, relaxation should return to your body. Enjoy the feeling that follows and continue breathing evenly and slowly.

Guided imagery

Do you wish you had a technique that could help you ease both your mind and body within seconds and still be easy to perform? Then this will be a great strategy for you! Guided imagery is very effective for de-stressing, and also for developing a thick skin. It is also one of the relaxation techniques that have proven effective in treating social anxiety disorder.

I'm sure you're eager to try this out, so let me explain how it works so you can start practicing!

However, before we jump in, there are a few different ways you can do this. First, you can do this in a class with an instructor guiding you. You can also use a recording that guides you through the exercise. You can even choose to record your own audio and use it. Lastly, you can rely on your inner subconscious voice to tell you what to do. In all of the options, you must be guided by something - that is where it gets its name from. This guide tells you what to do and how to do it.

Now that you are familiar with the concept, let's walk through how you can start practicing it.

Get Comfortable

You need a quiet place and a relaxed position. You may choose to recline in a chair or stay in a cross-legged position.

Execute Diaphragmatic Breathing

While closing your eyes and focusing on your breath, breathe diaphragmatically as described earlier in this chapter. While doing this, imagine that you are breathing out stress and breathing in peace. Check that your chest and shoulders are not moving as you are breathing, but rather only your abdomen should be moving.

Pick a Scene that Suits You and Vividly Imagine It

A relaxed scene may be different things for different people. For some, it might be winning a lottery ticket and filling the garage with fast cars, or it might be spending quality time with loved ones. Whatever brings to mind a relaxed state for you, begin to imagine it vividly.

Perhaps you can recall the details of a very pleasing memory from years past, or you can choose to envision a scene from a movie or book you love. The bottom line here is that the memory you pull up is pleasing to you.

Immerse Yourself in the Sensory Details

Now that you are envisioning your perfect scene, you need to get into the moment. Try to get all of your senses involved in imagining the place. Imagine how it smells, what it feels like, and any other details, like the sound of rain on the roof or a crackling fire in the fireplace.

Relax

Now that you have a detailed image in your mind, using all of your senses, it is time to settle in and relax. While you are here, ensure that you are enjoying the scene and everything in it. Stay there for as long as it pleases you. While relaxing here, detach yourself from every stress and anxiety. When you've had your fill, and you decide it is time to return to reality, just count down from twenty and maintain that feeling of serenity when you finish your countdown.

Mindfulness Techniques for Staying Present in Social Situations

We've seen how social anxiety can interrupt your life. But we've also seen that it doesn't have to be. You can stand up to it and reclaim your life. And one of the relaxation weapons in your arsenal is mindfulness. Mindfulness has immense power that you can use to ease social anxiety. Little wonder traditional Buddhists believe in it so much. Health professionals are actively using the power of relaxation, mindfulness, and meditation to help treat several health conditions like anxiety, depression, pain, insomnia, and even post-traumatic stress disorder.

How about athletes who use the principles of relaxation to better their performances? Or CEOs of big firms who use its principles to keep their cool in the chaotic world of business? Relaxation techniques such as mindfulness and meditation are even finding their way into the school curriculum these days, as students and teachers are shown how to use it to control their emotions and improve their concentration.

What is mindfulness? Think of it like this: have you ever been in a really noisy environment, and you somehow manage to tune out all of the noise and focus on what was important to you, perhaps a book you were in the middle of? If yes, that was the power of mindfulness. You simply streamlined your mind to pay attention to that which was most important to you.

However, to use mindfulness for managing social anxiety, it is slightly different. If you have ever tried to avoid a negative thought before, then you know how difficult that can be. It is difficult because as you are trying to block off such thoughts, the brain assumes that thought is very important and actually holds on to it. So when we are using mindfulness for social anxiety, we are not trying to block off those unpleasant thoughts such as "I'm not good enough" or "they don't like me" or "I will embarrass myself." Instead, what we are trying to do is to recognize the existence of these thoughts, and still convince ourselves that they are not helpful to us - because they truly are not! So, rather than focusing on those negative thoughts, we treat them like the noise in the aforementioned example, and we focus on the conversation or the task at hand.

Let's talk about the definition of mindfulness. Mindfulness is the ability to gather your thoughts into the present, even in a social situation. It is the ability to notice and focus on one's thoughts and feelings, without being judgmental about them. What does that mean for you? It means you are letting go of the thoughts of whether you are good enough or not, and you are focusing on the present, without any form of distraction.

Below are a few mindfulness techniques you can use to ease symptoms of social anxiety.

Become aware that you are anxious

Let me ask you, how are you going to take action to kick out your anxiety if you are not aware that you are anxious? The key is recognizing this feeling. Thankfully, we have gone through the symptoms of social anxiety in the second chapter of this book. You can go over them and identify the symptoms that apply for you so that you have a better understanding of when you're feeling anxious. When you recognize it, you can then begin applying these hacks to ease it.

Blame the anxiety, not yourself

If you realize that you are suffering from social anxiety, don't blame yourself. Instead of that, shift the blame to the actual cause of your condition… the social anxiety disorder. Then try to take back control. Try to see the disorder as a foreign element that has come to bother you, and put up your defenses. Remind yourself that you, and you alone, get to decide how you feel. Then fall back on any of the techniques we've discussed so far.

Focus on your senses by using the "Remember the Five" technique

This technique is a mindfulness strategy that can help you deal with anxiety, distractions, and overwhelming thoughts. Whenever you find yourself becoming overwhelmed, use the "remember the five" technique to bring your mind to the present.

What is it all about? This exercise is aimed at attaching your senses to your current situation or environment.

To do it, stop whatever you are doing, close your eyes, and take a deep breath. Then, with your eyes closed, try to remember five items in your immediate surroundings. Not just the items, try to remember their shapes, their sizes, what they are made of, the color, and other things any other details you can recall. You have attended to your sense of sight.

Next, move on to your sense of sound. Try to differentiate five different sounds you are currently hearing. Are there cars on the street, maybe kids playing outside, or music? Get detailed - what type of music is it? What do the cars sound like as they pass?

Engage your sense of touch by trying to feel five things, like your clothing, your hands on your lap, or your feet on the floor.

With your senses engaged, linger in the moment. With the conclusion of this exercise, hopefully, you have freed your mind and released some tension.

Focus your attention outward

Remember how you typically focus all your attention on yourself when you are in a social setting? That is not good for your anxiety. Rather than bothering yourself over what other people may think about you or how you are going to embarrass yourself, shift your attention outward. You could decide to listen to the music playing down the hall, or to pay attention to the beautiful decorations around you, or better yet, the people you are meeting. By doing this, you are becoming more mindful of your environment, and less about the pressure you're putting on yourself. At first it may not be easy, but with practice, you will see improvement.

Don't get me wrong, I am not saying your anxiety will magically grow wings and fly away. Those feelings will be there, but they will be less powerful because you will be able to classify them as background noises. Even though you will acknowledge that they are there, you will not pay attention to them.

If you are finding it hard to be present and active in your environment, come up with a cliché that you can say to snap you out of your thoughts. For example, if you are meeting a new person and the anxiety starts to bubble up, snap out of it by telling yourself "focus," or any other word of your choosing that will remind you to stay present.

In this chapter, I discussed the different relaxation techniques you can use to prevent anxiety in social situations and how to use them. In the next chapter, I will be discussing people-pleasing, how it affects you, and ways to stop.

CHAPTER SIX:

Stop People-Pleasing

People-pleasing is so common that you might even mistake it for politeness. You might think, "I'm just being nice." But that way of thinking is how you will always find yourself saying "yes" when all you want to do is shout "no!"

I know that feeling because I have been there before, and, trust me, it is not a nice place to be. If you are like me, then you know that people-pleasing can rob you of your peace of mind, and it can also contribute to depression and anxiety.

If you are a people pleaser, then I am sure you will relate to the description above. However, there are many other signs of people-pleasing. Let's look at some of them.

Am I a People Pleaser?

I know that's the question you're asking yourself right now. The next few sentences of this book will answer that for you. Funnily enough, you can be a people pleaser and not know it. As I mentioned earlier, you may mistake it for kindness or politeness.

Here are some common habits that suggest you are a people pleaser:

- You find it difficult to say "no."
- You find it difficult to voice your opinions and stand your ground.
- You're very sensitive to perceived rejection from others, even when it is not there.
- You're afraid of negative emotions.
- You're altruistic or philanthropic to a fault.
- You allow yourself to suffer at the expense of others.
- You lack personal boundaries.
- Relationships make you emotionally dependent.
- You live on other people's approval, always wanting it.
- You badly want to be liked by everyone.
- You hate criticism, and when it comes, you feel shattered for days.
- You have low self-esteem and self-worth.
- You are always conscious of what other people think of you, and you allow it to influence your actions.
- You can easily relate to other people's predicaments, often at your own expense.
- You always want to believe that other people are fair, even when it is clear they are abusive to you.
- You fear you might lose control over yourself.
- You help everyone you come across, even if you don't like them
- You hardly ever ask for or receive help.
- You are constantly apologizing even when you haven't done anything wrong.
- You easily attract people who need consolation.
- You have a constant fear of hurting people's feelings.
- You don't give yourself credit for anything.
- You believe that you are less than other people.
- You agree with people even when what they are saying is against your personal beliefs.
- You avoid telling others that they've hurt your feelings.

Where Does It Come from?

There is not a single, definite cause for people-pleasing. The condition stems from a combination of several factors, such as:

Past trauma

If you have suffered trauma before, you can have certain fears associated with the trauma. People-pleasing behaviors can surface as a response. People who have been victims of abuse may lose self-esteem or boundaries due to the experience.

Having a Low Self-esteem

The messages you got from people around you when you were growing up can greatly impact your self-esteem. If your self-esteem is low, you will be seeking approval, and you will become a people pleaser in the process.

Fear of rejection

If you have been rejected before by people, you may start to feel that you are no good, and other people will be likely to reject you, too. You may develop people-pleasing behaviors to avoid rejection again.

How Does it Affect You?

You may be saying, "Oh come on, I'm just being nice… maybe a little too much, but how does that negatively affect me?" Many ways. Let me show you some of them.

1. You suppress your emotions

When you are seeking the approval of people around you, you won't say anything that might ruin your chances of approval, so you may find yourself bottling up your emotions. These bottled up emotions can degenerate to damaging emotions such as rage, bitterness, grief, and anxiety. When you continue to suppress emotions, you are headed for either a physical, or psychological breakdown, or even both.

2. You put extreme pressure on yourself

Once you have started it, you must continue it. It's called "keeping up appearances." At first, when you couldn't say "no" to that request (even when it was too much for you), you thought you were being nice. But now that you have started it, you still can't say "no," and this just ends up piling up pressure on you because you want to maintain the selfless image you have created for yourself.

What do you get when you are struggling to keep up appearances? Nothing but stress. You might be thinking that it will make you feel good because you are putting yourself in people's good graces by doing them favors, but it is coming at the expense of your well-being. It's like wearing a mask for too long just to get other people's approval even when this mask is suffocating you.

3. People will use you

You may not know it yet, but there are a lot of bad people out there hiding in the name of friends, families, and acquaintances. We know them as narcissists, bullies, naysayers, energy vampires, and a host of other words. If you are a people pleaser, you will become an easy target for these people. You are an easy target because your nature makes it difficult for you to have personal boundaries, and you have an unquenchable desire to please people. This makes you a perfect item for use and abuse, and these people don't have boundaries, either. It is very difficult for you to get out because your life is dependent on approval. So the toxic cycle just continues.

4. No one knows your true nature

On the surface, this might seem appealing... "Oh, that's great, I will be unpredictable and invincible...." Before you start rejoicing about how you can be invincible and enigmatic by being unknown, hear me out. If no one truly knows who you are, you are lonely and disconnected. Trust me; this is not good for you, especially if you have social anxiety.

This is exactly what people-pleasing does to you. As a people pleaser, you will always put on the façade, and it is this façade that people around will know, and not the real you. Your original intention for putting up the façade is to get people's acceptance, but what you will get is disconnection. Where is the wisdom in that?

5. You won't enjoy relationships

Relationships are all about give and take. But as a people pleaser, some of your relationships are better captioned as "give and give." The people you are in a relationship with are only with you because of what you offer them. How on earth are you going to enjoy such a relationship? But being a people pleaser, you will just be suffering and smiling, because you want their approval.

6. Your friends and partners will find you frustrating

People who are close to you, such as a spouse, might notice how you do inexplicable things like apologize incessantly, and since they truly love you, it might start getting to them. Then, you can also fall into the common trap of sacrificing the time that should go into your relationships for pleasing others. Also, in some cases, you might lie to the people you love just because you want to spare their feelings, and they find out, it usually doesn't end well.

Ways to Stop People-Pleasing

I can hear you saying, "I've read enough already; show me how I can put a stop to people-pleasing!"

1. Seek internal validation

A people pleaser seeks outward approval and validation. If you can turn that around by validating yourself internally, then half the battle is won. But how can you validate yourself internally? Simple, by building up what makes you happy about yourself. If you are happy all by yourself, you don't need to rely on people anymore for that. So, to fight people-pleasing, invest your time in building up whatever makes you feel good. If you are already feeling good with yourself, do you still need people to make you feel good? Engage in those activities that make you feel great. If you love partying, by all means, attend parties often. If it is gardening that you love, set up and run a garden. Just do those things that make you feel good about yourself. Whenever you catch yourself craving external validation, knock it off by reminding yourself that you have a lot going for you.

2. Start small

When you were a toddler, you didn't just stand up one day and run across the sitting room, did you? You started with one or two baby steps. The same applies to stopping people-pleasing. Don't try to slam on the brakes and jolt yourself to a full stop on day one. If you do so, you will make a lot of enemies. So instead of suddenly refusing all new requests (where you previously would always say "yes"), try out saying yes, but doing a little of the request, not all. For instance, if a friend has just invited you to a party at a very inconvenient time of your life, you can go, stay a few minutes and return home.

3. Allow yourself time

Before now, your usual response to requests was an impulsive "yes" that you didn't give much thought. Try changing that by giving yourself time. Instead of just accepting requests, say something that can give you a little time to consider it, and decide if it is something you can do. You can prepare a default answer such as "Let me get back to you." or "let me check my schedule." or "let me check with my spouse." After some time, look for a way to politely say "no" to those requests that are out of order. If it is going to be difficult for you to say "no" to the person's face, you can choose to do that via email or text.

Two realizations that can help you learn how to say no without guilt are:

- You are not responsible for the happiness and comfort of people around you, they are responsible for theirs, and you are responsible for yours.
- You are expected to cater to yourself first before catering to others. So if anything is going to please someone at your expense, then it is a no-no.

4. **Know your principles, priorities, and boundaries and stand by them**

A person without these things is a pushover. You'll go along with anything you are told if you have no principles of your own. And if you lack boundaries, people can infringe upon you any time they want. Make sure you know your principles, priorities, and boundaries, and most importantly, ensure that the people around you know of your principles and boundaries.

5. **Remove toxic people**

Also, surround yourself with people that make you feel good about yourself, even without wanting anything from you. I know how difficult it is to remove toxic people from your life. Most of them are tightly woven into your family, circle of friends, or career. In such cases, it becomes more difficult, but you can manage them using the steps below:

- First of all, don't expect them to change. Toxic people have complex problems and desires of their own. Toxic people often believe that they are right, and you are wrong. So, realize that you can wish that they will change, but your wish cannot do it. Your efforts too cannot do it lest you lose yourself while trying to save them from themselves.
- Now that you have realized that they will not change, it is time to set some boundaries that you must maintain. If you don't set boundaries, toxic people will push you to extreme lengths. To do this, take time out to think about what you want from your friends, coworkers, families, and acquaintances. Keep them top of mind or write them down if need be. If, at any point in your interaction with toxic people, you feel that something is off, cross-check it with your boundaries and be prepared to enforce them if they are being infringed on.
- Don't allow yourself to be pulled into crises that they deliberately create. Toxic people have a way of inducing crises so that they will get your sympathy and attention. You may feel that you are being a good Samaritan, however, you are allowing yourself to pick up negative energy. When they create drama and

expect to get you entangled in it, remember that it is not a genuine distress call in order to maintain perspective.

- Understand your weaknesses and difficulties so that toxic people will not use it against you. They look for weaknesses in you and exploit them. For instance, they might notice that you are somebody who cannot just watch people suffer. Because of that, they will paint a nasty picture of them almost dying whenever they need a favor from you. But if you have realized that this is your area of weakness, you will easily notice when people are trying to exploit it.
- Realize that toxic people might resist your efforts to thwart their tactics. If you've had a toxic person in your life before, then you know they can easily throw tantrums whenever they feel ignored. When they sense that you are developing a resilience to their tactics, they may increase their efforts, and you may be tempted to give in. Instead, realize that it is normal for them to act that way. Continue with your defensive tactics, and when they see that they can no longer control you, they will leave your life and seek a place where they can satisfy their selfish intentions. At this stage, you can congratulate yourself knowing that you are free from toxicity.

6. Stop apologizing

Apologizing when you are in the wrong isn't bad. It's when you were not in the wrong and apologizing becomes second nature.

If you are to blame for something and you give a heartwarming apology, there is nothing wrong with that. But if you are always on the apologizing end, even when it is very clear that you are not to blame - that is what is wrong, and you need to stop it as soon as you finish reading this book.

Let me give you a scenario, as a people pleaser. I've done my fair share of apologizing when it was not my fault. Some time ago, my boss had asked me to place an order for lunch for the workers in the firm. I promptly did, sticking to his instruction of "gluten-free." But then when the order came, it turned out that the restaurant had messed up. It was not my fault, because I was sure of what I ordered, and it was even clearly written on the receipt, but I still felt bad because some workers could not eat it. I ended up apologizing to whoever would listen, as if it were my own doing.

You might be tempted to say, "You apologized, what's the big deal?" The truth is that whenever you apologize for something, you are indirectly accepting blame and heaping pressure on yourself. Somewhere deep down, your mood is affected by something you are innocent of.

Scenarios like this portray how fragile we (people pleasers) can be. But I've long gone past that, and I know you will be ready to make the transition when you finish this chapter.

Here are some tips that can help you apologize only when it is necessary:

Assessment: don't be quick to rush into an apology, take a short time to assess and appraise the situation. Ask yourself, "Am I responsible for this?" or "Is there something I could have done differently to avoid this?" If your answers to these two questions is an emphatic "No," please don't take the blame and apologize.

Conclusively, it is also important that I say this. Even though you are trying to put a stop to people-pleasing, it doesn't mean that you should transform into a cold-hearted monster. We still need touches of humanity here and there. Know where the difference lies between being nice and being a people pleaser.

Being a people pleaser just to feel approval or avoid getting your opinion out there will only hurt your self-esteem and make you more anxious in social situations. In this chapter, I explained what it means to be a people pleaser, how it affects your life, and how to stop being a people pleaser. In the next chapter, I will be discussing shyness; what causes it, how it can affect you, and ways you can cure your shyness.

CHAPTER SEVEN:

Cure Your Shyness

All of us have been shy at one point or another. When moderate, you can still say or do what you want, even though you are slightly shy. If you can still be yourself, it is normal. But with certain people, that is not the case. These people with extreme shyness issues are always incapacitated due to the extreme apprehension they feel whenever they are around people. They cannot be in the midst of people without feeling very awkward. It is strongly believed to be a result of low self-esteem. It is fueled by your fear of what other people think of you. Since you are overly concerned about what people think about you, you will become scared that you might be humiliated, rejected, or criticized. So to avoid the possibility of any of these happening, shy people will avoid every social situation.

It can be even stronger in people with a social anxiety disorder. This extreme shyness will trigger all the symptoms we've discussed earlier in this book. Humans are social animals, meaning that we thrive among other people. So if you allow a thing like shyness to make you avoid people, you need to do something about it.

Some Facts on Shyness

- **Shyness is dependent on age**, meaning that you can be shy as a child, and when you grow into an adult and experience new things, you also outgrow it.

- **Shyness can come and go**. You can go in and out of periods of shyness, depending on what is going on in your life at those times. If you are in a phase of your life where you are seriously battling with self-confidence, the chances are that you will be more shy. When you bounce back and reclaim your confidence, the shyness is reduced.
- **Shyness is closely related to self-consciousness**. People who are very conscious of themselves are more likely to be shy. Shyness is also closely linked to fear. So people who were fearful in childhood are more likely to end up as shy adults.

What Causes Shyness?

Just like people-pleasing, there is not a single particular cause for shyness. Rather, it is caused by a combination of different factors cutting across nature and nurture.

One thing that we know for sure is there is not a gene for shyness. It is not hereditary, you didn't get it from either of your parents or somebody in your family line. So it is natural occurrences that influence you to be shy or not. Some of the most common occurrences are when you are treated too harshly as a child, when you have a faulty perception of yourself, or when you undergo some life transitions that are difficult for you to handle, like getting a new job, going to a new school, or getting a divorce.

Let us look at some of the factors that can contribute to shyness:

Before you can cure shyness effectively, you need to understand where it comes from. For instance, it might be something in your past that injured your self-image and left you shy. It could be a very damaging personal belief you hold about yourself. If you succeed in identifying the cause, half the battle is won.

Therefore, let us take a little time to look at the possible cause of your shyness. They include:

- **Lack of self-confidence:** When your self-esteem is low, you are overly critical of yourself, and so you will believe that people see you the way you see yourself. To try and shield yourself from their negative review, you become shy.
- **Inferiority complex:** When you feel like you are the lowest person in the room, you will be very reluctant to speak up or express yourself because you've convinced yourself that you don't have anything to offer.
- **Perfectionism:** If you are an extreme perfectionist, you will always want to say and do impeccable things. And because you don't want to make any mistakes at all, you will just choose to keep to yourself and shyness kicks in.
- **Lack of social skills:** We've seen the clamor surrounding the inclusion of social skills in schools. This is because several people go through school without picking these up. When you lack social skills, you will become self-inhibited. And since you don't know how to socialize with people, you will end up keeping to yourself and being shy.
- **Faulty self-image:** If you have any degrading thoughts about yourself, you will end up being shy because a bad self-image will lead you to self-inhibition.
- **Undue fear of people:** If you've been a subject of abuse or you come from a dysfunctional family, you might be scared of people, and that can make you shy.

Effects of Shyness

It can slow your learning in an academic environment

If you are or have been a student before, then you know that one key ingredient for success in schools is your ability to interact with others and participate in group tasks. If you are shy, it can hamper that and reduce your performance and grades. This can even affect your self-confidence and make you perform below your actual abilities.

It slows down your career growth

The job market these days is very competitive, and only the strong survive. If you are shy, you may not be able to get a good job because you falter in the interview stages, and no company is looking to add liability to their workforce. Let's say you somehow get in; you won't be able to give good presentations that can earn you your boss' approval. You won't be able to speak up in meetings, and you will lose that opportunity to show how thoughtful and promotion-deserving you are.

Difficulties forming relationships

Extreme shyness can make you a loner. Since you are mostly shy when you are around others, you may prefer to just keep to yourself, and that is how you will not have good friends you can share things with.

Ways to Overcome Shyness

I think you have seen enough reason why you should cure yourself of that shyness today. If you haven't, let me summarize it for you. In a nutshell, shyness can hold you back from doing things that can be beneficial to you. It can also pile stress and anxiety on you, especially when you are in the midst of people.

But, I have good news for you. The first one is that you are not alone. Out of every ten people, four of them will agree that they are shy.

The second piece of good news I have for you is that no matter how shy you might consider yourself, you can overcome it. All it will take is time and effort, and you will see yourself breaking free from the grip of shyness.

I have compiled some techniques for you that you can use in your fight against shyness. These are techniques that have proven effective to countless people before you. If you can discipline yourself to follow them judiciously, you will see results in no time.

Plan ahead

You can plan by first identifying your triggers. Know those situations that make you shy and make accurate plans for them when you anticipate them. Decide on what to do when the situation presents itself, if possible, write your steps down. Most people are triggered by public speaking, while others have some more specific triggers such as a person, a song, or a venue. Be sure you know your triggers and plan for them.

Be curious and get informed

If you have an upcoming event where you are likely going to meet new people, you might want to arm yourself with some conversation starters. Get to know the new trends in technology, politics, business, or entertainment... whatever suits you. Check for the trending topics on social media and arm yourself with pieces of it. That way you will have something to say. And when you say something, and it passes off as smart, and people are digging it, you will feel comfortable saying more. Remember to keep your cool. These people don't even know that you are shy and you don't have to let them know. While doing this, remember that your intention is not to impress them with how much you know, you are just blending in and having good conversation.

Be kind to yourself

Most of the mental challenges, including shyness, are not cured by a snap of the fingers. They require a considerable amount of time and effort to go away. While you are working on your shyness, if you do not see drastic improvements, go easy on yourself. What is important is that you are making the effort, and you are making progress, even though you may not have noticed it. Don't concentrate too much on your pace, just concentrate on making the effort, no matter how small.

Be confident and act confident

Whenever we start learning a new task, our confidence will be low at first, but as we continue to practice, our confidence begins to rise. It was like that when you learned to drive a car, or ride a bicycle. The same applies to relating to people. You are shy because you lack confidence. But what if you can learn to be confident... by being confident? If you can start speaking confidently and acting confidently, you will notice that it feels good, and you will become more confident with the process. When you are feeling shy and anxious, the anxiety is not the problem; the real problem is that you are avoiding social interactions. If you can be confident enough to eliminate the avoidance, the anxiety will melt away.

Engage more

Remember that your shyness and anxiety increase as the number of people around you increases. You can handle a one-on-one conversation, but you wouldn't talk to a group. So why not start from smaller conversations and grow? To do this, initiate small talks, strike up random conversations with strangers at the gym, the grocery, the subway, or worship centers. Just get talking. As you do this more often, your confidence will grow. For even more improvement, talk to people you find attractive, ask them for a date, or a dance. Hearing someone say "yes" to you will begin to reorient the image you have about yourself. If you do get a "no" - shake it off and move on. Of the seven billion people on earth, not everyone will like you. But more than half will. So don't waste energy. Just go out more and meet new people.

Try new things, even if you are not comfortable with it

Clubs, sports teams, and classes are good places you can consider. This will allow you to meet new people and socialize more. You can also consider embarking on those projects you have always been wanting to do, but your shyness has held you back. You can decide to learn a new skill or undertake a difficult project. By all means, get out of your comfort zone and meet people.

You might be wondering how taking on difficult tasks can alleviate shyness. When you undertake a difficult task and come through with it, you feel better about yourself and your self-confidence surges. To eliminate shyness, you will have to develop confidence in various aspects of your life.

Also, when you try new activities, you are confronting the unknown, and you are eliminating anxiety by doing so because we feel anxious about the unknown.

Start talking

In my experience, I think that the anxiety we experience as shy people is usually at its peak when we have to stand before a group of people and make a speech. We call it "stage fright," but it is still shyness dressed in a different outfit. So to start confronting your shyness, I recommend joining a speech club. While there, take on speeches and presentations. Do it even when your mind and body are against it. Also, whenever you have an opportunity to address a crowd, embrace it! Don't be scared of doing badly. At first, you might, but as time goes on, your confidence will grow, and you will begin to unravel the seemingly herculean task. Even when you are with your friends and coworkers, make your opinion known often, speak up and try to be more talkative. As a shy person, what you consider as talkative may be another person's normal.

One attribute of confident people is that they don't care whether people will like what they have to say. They say it nonetheless because they are more concerned with connecting and sharing. And oftentimes they are confident of what they have to say. You can emulate that.

Additional note on shyness:

Some of you reading this book may be parents. You can help your children overcome shyness at an early stage. There are indications that shyness can be corrected early in one's life using social development. Unfortunately, this has never been a top priority in homes and schools. In homes, many parents can be overprotective, as they try to keep their children away from social settings. Schools, on the other hand, focus more on reading and writing, and they forget to help children develop the necessary social skills that can help them be better people when they grow up. Certain children show signs of withdrawal at an early age. If teachers and parents can pay attention to such children and model social skills and help encourage them to express themselves more and interact with other kids, they can eliminate the impending shyness.

To prevent shyness in your kids, you can help them develop the vital skills that will help them be more comfortable with their peers. These skills include:

- Showing them how to cope with change.
- Teaching them how to manage their anger.
- Treating them to a healthy dose of compassion and humor.
- Teaching them how to be assertive and have a voice of their own.
- Teaching them how to show kindness and help others.
- Teaching them how to keep secrets, when appropriate.

In this chapter, I explained how you can overcome your shyness and learn how to speak up around others. In the next chapter, I will be discussing social confidence, the benefits of having good social confidence, and how you can build your social confidence.

CHAPTER EIGHT:

How to Build Social Confidence

We have covered so much through the course of this book. And now, everything is beginning to come together. We've talked about social anxiety, and how you can rid yourself of it. We also looked at shyness, and how to stop it. We looked at people-pleasing, and how to overcome it. All of these topics are aimed at doing one critical thing, and that is to help you overcome the shyness and anxiety you experience whenever you are in a social setting. In a nutshell, all we've been doing is building your social confidence so that you do not become anxious, shy, or tense.

The topics we've discussed so far will improve your social life by improving your social confidence, but in this chapter, I want to give you practical tips that you can use to further improve your social confidence.

Before I show you the ways you can build your social confidence, let me motivate you by showing you what you stand to gain.

Benefits of Good Social Confidence

More friends, more fun

For us socially challenged people, sometimes we like to believe that nothing is better than the comfort of our bed, our computer and our favorite couch in the house. Nothing could be further from the truth. Life begins where social anxiety ends. If you are not socializing, you are not meeting people, and that is sad because people make life more fun and worth living. Our families, friends, and coworkers make life more fun. So much fun awaits you when you finally reclaim your social confidence.

Excellence in career and school

Schools and work environments are also social situations. And if you can't function very well in other social situations, how then will you be able to perform well in these? The obvious answer is that you can't. To truly make any headway in school or your career, you need good social confidence.

Freedom from shyness

Think about the last party you attended. The one where you sat alone in the corner, hoping that someone will come by and say hello… Why did that happen? Is it that you just found that particular spot cozy, or did you have a more cogent reason for keeping all to yourself? I think I might know why you opted for the option you chose; you simply didn't feel confident enough to socialize. If you had good social confidence, maybe you would have been the life of that party. A lack of social confidence is equal to shyness, and you've seen the negative impacts shyness can have on you.

Freedom from people-pleasing

We've discussed people-pleasing in this book, and I believe that you saw the debilitating effects it can have on you. I explained that it comes from your inner desire to be validated by others, and that you are often seeking that validation because you are not confident about yourself. But when you finally achieve social confidence, all of that changes. You no longer need to go out of your way for validation.

The points above are just a few examples of what social confidence can do for you. Now, let's see how you can build this all-important attribute from the ground up. No matter how low you've previously been with your social confidence, the steps below can help you get started.

Ways to Begin Building Social Confidence

To build good social confidence, you'll need to make changes to several aspects of your life. You'll have to create a confident outlook; improve your confidence, social skills, and practice confidence.

So we'll group our discourse into the three parts.

Creating a Confident Outlook

1. **Accept yourself the way you are**

You need to first accept your introverted nature and be in love with it. Accepting yourself the way you are is good for your self-image. Regardless of the buzz surrounding socializing, quiet and personal time is still priceless. Rather than suddenly hating who you are and trying to make an abrupt switch, learn to love the person you are. If you try to make that abrupt switch, it could lead to more stress and anxiety. A better way to make the transition is to focus on the social situations you are already comfortable with. Focus on improving the quality of the social interactions you have going for you. If you enjoy meeting and playing board games with a group of close friends, focus on improving the quality of the conversation and interaction that goes on there. Stay there and unwind before moving on to bigger things.

2. **Do away with negative beliefs and thoughts**

The second best thing for you is to avoid those thought patterns that can render your efforts null and void. Avoid thoughts like, "I am boring," or "I don't fit in," or even "I just can't socialize." These thought patterns buried deep in your subconscious will create your reality. For instance, imagine you are on a date and you are so busy telling yourself that you are boring, and they won't like you. What do you think will happen? You will end up being boring. Once everything in you has accepted that you are truly boring, you are definitely going to bore your date to death.

Once you have accepted that you are boring, you will start looking for evidence that confirms your belief. Even when these pieces of evidence are meaningless coincidences, you will just take them as clear confirmation of your suspicion. The result? Further pressure on yourself. So always try to reframe your mind from having such negative thoughts.

3. Let your expectations be realistic

You might know this already, but let me say it again. Not everyone will like you, and it is not everybody that you will like... you won't vibe with everyone. So don't fall apart because you tried to relate with just one or two people and it didn't happen. Tell yourself that you both don't click, and that's normal. So if you try to initiate a conversation with a stranger and they ignore you, it is not you, it's them too... shrug it off. Who knows what they might be battling with!

Creating a confident outlook also entails cutting yourself some slack. Let me show you a few steps to do that.

- Don't take yourself too seriously

One of the primary reasons for low social confidence is too much awareness. When you care too much about how you look, how you dress, how you walk, it is an indication that you are taking yourself too seriously, and it doesn't always end well. If you are the type of person that also cares too much about other people's opinions of you, just chill and realize that people have the liberty to their opinions, and you have no control over it.

Stop being judgmental on yourself. We've seen how judging yourself can lead to social anxiety and shyness. It can also negatively impact your social confidence. Cut yourself some slack and take a breath. For instance, if you find out that you are always judging what you say, try this: Quit filtering your words and just speak, because often, you have a thousand and one reasonable things to say, you are just being too careful.

- Don't give a crap

Try not to care so much. Apply the principles we talked about in the people-pleasing chapter of this book. Set your priorities and honor them.

Improving Yourself and Your Social Skills

We have two segments to this section. The first is improving every area of your life, and the other is improving your social skills.

For improving every area of your life, it is quite simple. Just be the best version of yourself. If you've always wanted to do away with that belly fat and get yourself a ripped body, hit the gym and get it done. If you've always wanted to be in a ballet class dancing to a beautiful symphony, by all means, sign up and get dancing. Whatever it is that will make your life more desirable, get it done. The idea is that when you have achieved the best version of yourself, your confidence level will naturally improve.

Now let's look at the other aspect, improving your social skills.

I cannot overemphasize the need for you to improve your social skills. Don't just look forward to socializing, spend time to prepare yourself for it. Some social skills you can look to develop are:

1. Knowing how to show interest in people

If you can master the skills of making people feel loved, valued, and wanted, they will naturally gravitate towards you. It is known as social competency, and it passes for social confidence, too. There are subtle non-verbal signals you can use to make people feel wanted. Some of these nonverbal signals are:

- Maintaining eye contact and having the right facial expressions.
- Sitting up tall and widening your chest.
- Smile always, as a way of letting them know you welcome them.
- When taking a posture, choose a still one. Ensure you are neither swaying nor fidgeting.
- Let your handshakes be firm.

2. Speak clearly and at a reasonable pace

Don't just mumble your words, and don't rush through it like it is a difficult task. Calm down and try to speak at a rate that people can easily understand. Apart from having more effective communication, this also portrays confidence. If at any point in your conversation, you notice that you are mumbling or speeding up, pause your statement, take a deep breath and try again. While doing this, don't let any of it show.

3. Be an effective listener

People are naturally drawn to those who can listen to and understand them. You can strategically position yourself to make lots of friends if you master the art of listening effectively. Don't just listen, listen with intent. You intend to come up with the most suitable and thoughtful response possible. To do this, you will need to remove your attention from yourself and focus it on others. Focusing your attention on them does two things for you. First, it removes the tension from you, and secondly, it endears you to others because it tells them that you care about them.

4. Practicing confidence

It is not just enough for you to know the theories on improving social confidence, discipline yourself to apply them in your everyday life.

Let's look at some steps you can take to practice social confidence:

- Expose yourself to the actual social situations

No matter the number of steps I give you on how to improve your social confidence, your confidence can only improve as you flex your confidence muscles. You can do that by exposing yourself to real social situations. As you try it, you become more confident. With this increasing confidence, your anxiety will begin to wane.

- Role play

If it is difficult for you to just get into social situations, you can start with role play. Have a trusted friend be the stranger and practice social skills with them. Focus on learning how to introduce yourself, start a conversation, and sustain it for a while.

- Socialize with the help of a friend

When starting your social freedom journey, consider going out with a friend or relative you are very comfortable around. Their presence can help you because you will realize you are not just among strangers. You came along with your good buddy, who will have your back any time.

There we have them; steps you can take to push your social confidence to heights you never thought possible.

In this chapter, I gave different tips you can use in building your social confidence and how to use them. In the next chapter, we will be taking it to the next level by learning how to improve your self-esteem.

CHAPTER NINE:

Improving Your Self Esteem

There is nothing more important than how we think and feel about ourselves. One of the things most people miss in our society is having a high opinion of one's self, who we are, what we do, and the love we have for ourselves.

In a few words, self-esteem is an opinion of oneself and their abilities. This opinion can be low, high, or somewhere in between. Despite having occasional doubts about oneself, having low self-esteem can be damaging, leaving you to feel unmotivated and insecure. Your reason for having low self-esteem may vary. You might be able to point out some of the specific things that affect how you see yourself (like bullying), or it could remain a mystery to you.

Having low self-esteem can be an unfortunate self-fulfilling prophecy because feeling worse about what you do and who you are makes it less motivating to do what it takes to boost your self-esteem. It now becomes easy to spiral down into a cycle of circular and negative thinking. This creates damaging, mired, and wrong beliefs, which aren't ideal, especially if you have a social anxiety disorder.

Either way, there are still things you can do to improve your self-esteem. Improving your self-esteem is a process that doesn't happen overnight. However, there are some things you can do to get started and speed up the process.

Tips for Improving Your Self Esteem

Below are some helpful tips you can use to improve your self-esteem. Everyone has it, and having access to the right tip will go a long way.

Master A New Skill

As humans, we are always learning on a near-constant basis, and considering how the world is evolving, we are left with little or no choice but to adapt to what the world brings. Mastering a new skill can help you a lot, especially within the work and school environments.

Due to the learning process involved in acquiring a new skill, you will not only have a new skill to your name but have the privilege to take on new tasks when necessary, increasing your sense of competency. You become more proactive and have the ability to talk on subjects that you didn't have any ideas about before. Overall, this will change how you see yourself and make you place more value on yourself over time.

Be Nice To Yourself

It is so typical of us to damage our self-esteem further by being self-critical. That shouldn't be the case; we must learn how to be nice to ourselves. That voice in your head that keeps reminding you that you are failing is more powerful than you realize, instead of allowing it to take control of your life, be kind to yourself, and challenge any negative thoughts.

A good way to keep this in check is always to treat yourself how you treat others. If you are very respectful and listen to what others have to say, learn to also do the same for yourself. Speak to yourself the same way you would speak to your mates. At first, this may prove difficult, but after much practice, you will get better at it and eventually master being nice to yourself.

Be Yourself (Do You)

Do you know who you are? Are you being your true self? Since our childhood days, we have been conditioned to act in a certain way. Once you figure out who you are and learn how to be yourself, you will definitely be in a happier place.

Never aim to please others. It can be nice initially, but you need to know your boundaries. When you start comparing yourself with others, you will start feeling inferior and find it hard to be yourself. Instead, try to focus more on your achievements and goals and not measure them with that of someone else. That kind of pressure isn't healthy for anyone, and you don't need it in your life. Just be yourself!

Move More (Get Exercising)

According to a 2016 study, there is a correlation between exercise and having higher self-esteem, including improved mental health. (Sani, Fathirezaie, & Talepasand, 2016).

Debbie Mandel, the author of *Addicted to Stress* suggested that when you engage in physical activity, you are creating both mental and physical empowerment, especially weight lifting.

Exercising will help you organize your day around taking care of yourself. Find a way to squeeze in some time just to relax and do something fun – you will see how relaxing it feels. Other ways you can take care of yourself is by getting enough sleep, eating proper nutrition, and giving yourself a treat once in a while.

Know That Nobody is Perfect

No one has it all, no one is perfect in all they do, and everyone should know this. We all have our areas of strengths and weaknesses. Some of us are creative, others are not. Others are detail-oriented; some of us are not. No matter how hard you try, you can't be perfect.

Believing that there are perfect people can be destructive to your daily life, so refrain from such thoughts. It can hinder you from taking necessary actions because you will become too afraid that you are not living up to a particular standard. You will prefer to procrastinate and not get the results you want. This can really make your self-esteem go low.

Sometimes, there are certain actions you take that never satisfy you. You are never satisfied with your performance or accomplishments. By doing this, your feelings and opinions about yourself will keep being negative, and you will keep lacking the motivation to take action.

A few things that helped me realize my true self and know no one is perfect:

- Going for good enough. When you are trying to make yourself perfect because you are of the notion that there are perfect people, you begin to get yourself wound up and find it difficult to complete a task. Instead, go for just a simple good enough mentality. Although it shouldn't be an excuse for you to slack off, just realize that there is something called "good enough," and when you get there, you have completed your task.
- Keep in mind that subscribing to the myth of perfect people will only hurt you and the people in your life. This reminder should be able to make you see life as what it is and what it is not. Life isn't always what is portrayed in songs, books, movies, or social media. Have a reality check in place just in case you are developing the idea that you need to be perfect. Having the wrong perception can harm you and possibly make you lose potential projects, contracts, jobs, and even relationships.
- Everyone makes mistakes. To err is human, and we get to make mistakes to learn things and grow. So, whenever you make a mistake, never beat yourself up, instead, learn from it, and try again. You have definitely learned one or two things through the mistakes you made, and you get better with the next try.

Focus On the Things You Can Change

In the words of best-selling author and life-changing speaker, Steve Maraboli,

"Incredible change happens in your life when you decide to take control of what you so have power over instead of craving over what you don't"

You need to know the difference between the things you can control and those you can't. It is easy to get caught up with things that are totally out of your control, and this will prevent you from achieving much. Instead, focus your energy on the things you know are within your control and see what you can do about them.

When you focus on the things you can change, you don't worry too much because you know you are doing as much as you can for your happy and healthy space. It doesn't just free you from your anxiety; it also gives you a sense of deeper self-trust, which will boost your self-esteem.

Do What Makes You Happy

If you choose to do the things that make you happy, you are instantly improving your self-esteem. There won't be any room to sink into your insecurities as happiness trumps them all. People have low self-esteem because they believe all others say about them, not knowing that muting those words is a pathway to happiness.

When you spend more time doing the things you love and enjoy, you likely start thinking positively, and this can be contagious too. I have never heard of someone that regretted choosing to do the things that make them happy. Even if it doesn't go as they pictured it, the decision to do the things that make them happy leaves room for little regret.

You can try scheduling in a little time for yourself every day. Even if it is for cooking, being in the bath, lying on the couch, watching movies, or reading a book, just do something fun that you like. If it makes you happy, then it is worth it.

Celebrate Small Victories

Our society today has conditioned us to only care about celebrating big wins and breeze by the small ones. Even if it appears insignificant to celebrate small victories like cooking your favorite meal, waking up in the morning, starting a new project, being debt-free, or going for a long walk, they still need to be celebrated.

Celebrating your small wins is a great way of boosting your self-esteem. Realize that life isn't made up of just big moments, but the small ones. So start celebrating!

Be Helpful And Considerate To Other People

Being helpful to people has proven to be beneficial on so many levels. You not only get the satisfaction that you helped someone in need, but you also get an increased sense of purpose, which improves your self-esteem. Being helpful and considerate can increase your level of accessibility in your workplace and shape you into an asset the company wouldn't want to lose. So, try to focus on being considerate to people in your daily life. You can try doing any of the things below:

- Allow someone into your lane while driving, instead of blocking them off.
- When someone is trying to vent, just be there and listen to what he or she has to say.
- Be helpful to someone in a practical way, even if it's just for a few minutes.
- Hold the door for someone.
- You can be a motivator to a friend or family member that is feeling down and unmotivated.

Define What Success Means To You

We all want to be successful. We go after fame, money, power, relationships, and education all in the pursuit of success. Have you ever paused to ask yourself what success means to you? Only a few people will pause to find out what it means for them. If you don't define your life plan, there is a high chance of you falling into another person's plan, even when what they plan for you isn't much.

If you don't define success for yourself, you might end up climbing the wrong ladder, pursuing someone else's success, and you will only get to realize this after you have gotten to the top of the wrong mountain.

To define your success, you need to set your objectives, goals, and paths based on what you want, desire, and not what other people want for you. For some people, helping others brings them joy, so success for them is through giving to others. Try to tease out what success means to you. To do anything successfully, you need to find the self-esteem within yourself to get you there.

Surround Yourself With Supportive And Positive Squad

Positive people are real and not self-centered. They don't just care about themselves, but about others, too. With positivity follows authenticity, and you get to have people looking out for your well-being.

Always aim to surround yourself with positive people that will help bring out your full potential and help the world see the best version of you. Let go of any toxic and unsupportive friends you have and focus more on having a healthy squad.

You should know who treats you badly or tears you down instead of building you up. Despite this, you may find it difficult to avoid the toxic people around you because you feel you can't do without them or that you've known them for so long. What if keeping them close does greater harm than good?

It will be difficult to improve your self-esteem if what influences your life the most keeps dragging you down.

In order to make the necessary changes and get the desired results:

- Spend less of your time with people that are not kind, unsupportive, or perfectionists. They will never contribute anything good to your dreams or goals.

- Spend more of that time with people who are uplifting, supportive, and positive. These people have more humane, kinder, and better ways of thinking about the world.
- Think about the things you watch, read, and listen to. Use the time you spend on an internet forum to do other things if you feel it makes you doubt who you are, and have some negative feelings about yourself.
- Spend time listening to podcasts, reading books, websites, and blogs that will help you feel better about yourself.
- Avoid people that trigger you to become anxious or cause you to fall into negative thought patterns, and find people who will make you feel good about yourself.

Finally, as humans, we are all born with equal worth and countless potential. Having the belief that you are anything less is false, and I want you to drop it right now. By putting in hard work and practicing self-compassion, the self-destructive thoughts that often hinder your self-esteem from growing can be unlearned. All you need to do is to follow all I have outlined above and start increasing your self-worth. Everyone has it in them; you only need the right push to recognize it.

In this chapter, you learned what having self-esteem means and the different ways you can improve your self-esteem. Next, we will be going into the healing process (therapy). Once your anxiety is getting out of control, then therapy is the next thing to seek.

CHAPTER TEN:

Therapy for Social Anxiety

Social anxiety disorder (SAD) is a common psychiatric disorder. Though often labeled as shyness, it can create crippling fear that affects your work performance, school performance, social attendance, and relationships. Up to 12% of Americans will be affected by it in their lifetime.

Diagnosing social anxiety disorder can be hard, especially since it is confused with normal fear and shyness. This has caused a lot of people to not seek help. To make things easy, the *Diagnostic and Statistical Manual of Mental Disorders, Fourth Edition* has listed the criteria that can be used to diagnose a social anxiety disorder. It also describes how the disorder shows up in children and adults.

Almost half of the people with social anxiety disorder experience anxiety in certain situations, especially those situations that require public appearance and public speaking, while others have a generalized form of anxiety, which makes them experience fear in almost all kinds of social situations.

Though most people get nervous when speaking in front of a group or at parties, what differentiates it from a social anxiety disorder is the level of distress and damage it causes. For instance, research has suggested that adults with a social anxiety disorder are more likely to miss work, while a youth with the disorder are also more likely to drop out of high school. In fact, intimate relationships can be affected – which is a major reason people with a social anxiety disorder are less likely to marry early.

Still, because the symptoms of the disorder are often seen as minor, only half of the people with social anxiety disorder seek help or receive treatment. As I mentioned earlier, they typically experience the symptoms of SAD for at least ten years before seeking help. That is unfortunate because there are many treatments available that can help in reducing the symptoms of anxiety.

When To Seek Therapy For Social Anxiety

Have you been avoiding certain social situations for a few months? Have you been really stressed out because of this? If you are, then now is the time for you to seek help. If you always keep skipping events that you are interested in, but you are too scared to try it out, then it's time to seek help.

Similarly, you always assume you are not interested in things just because of that awkward feeling that comes with it. You know very well that you might find an activity fun, but you keep shoving it off and hiding behind cynicism.

If you have been finding it difficult to make new friends because going into a new environment sounds scary, or you see yourself being left alone while everyone is trying to mingle, or when someone tries to ask you out on a date, you have more than a million excuses for not going, you may have SAD. You keep pushing down the feeling of loneliness, telling yourself that it is what you are meant to live with.

Research has suggested that environmental and genetic factors interact to cause social anxiety. Though, to treat social anxiety, instead of focusing on why you have a problem, it will be beneficial to look at what is maintaining the anxiety and address the factors using cognitive behavioral therapy. Multiple research studies suggest that cognitive behavioral therapy (CBT) is an effective way of treating anxiety disorders, especially social anxiety disorders. All in all, the best way social anxiety disorder can be treated is through Cognitive Behavioral Therapy or medication. First, let's see what CBT is all about.

Cognitive Behavioral Therapy (CBT)

Cognitive Behavioral Therapy (CBT) is a common form of therapy that came into the limelight in the 1980s and 1990s for the treatment of anxiety disorders. According to research, CBT is a form of therapy that has consistently helped patients overcome their clinical anxiety disorders.

Cognitive Behavioral Therapy is not just a one-set method, but a combination of different techniques that depend on the particular anxiety disorder being treated. For instance, the CBT used for the treatment of social anxiety disorder is different from the one used in treating depression and other types of anxiety disorder.

Since there are so many different techniques of CBT, you must find a therapist who is experienced and knows the particular and most effective techniques for treating social anxiety disorder.

CBT aims to avail patients with techniques and practices so that the patients with social anxiety disorder can have new ways in which they think and behave in situations that seem terrifying to them. The therapy can be offered to an individual or to a group.

In exposure therapy, patients are exposed to the feared situation, and ways are suggested to help them manage the fear. For instance, if the school's upcoming prom night or the upcoming office party is already feeling overwhelming, a way to cope with this is to set an achievable goal, like starting a conversation with one or two people at the party. In the other variation of CBT, patients will practice and learn relaxation techniques and social skills to help them cope with anxiety. Though this isn't as well-studied as the exposure therapy.

Cognitive Behavioral Therapy usually consists of about twelve to sixteen weekly sessions that last for sixty to ninety minutes. Studies have suggested that patients with anxiety disorder go through six to twelve weeks of CBT before any visible improvement can be seen.

What CBT for Social Anxiety Entails

- Facing social situations that give you anxiety, gradually and efficiently, instead of avoiding the situation.
- Learning to control the physical symptoms associated with anxiety with the use of breathing exercises and relaxation techniques.
- Challenging unhelpful and negative thoughts that trigger and fuel your anxiety. Switch them with a more balanced view.
- Even though you can learn breathing exercises, relaxation, and relaxation techniques, you can also benefit from the guidance and extra support a therapist offers.

Goals of CBT for Social Anxiety Disorder

The major goal of CBT is to identify your irrational thoughts and beliefs and replace them with more realistic views. In the CBT process, you need to work on some areas, and they are:

- How to be more assertive
- Anger, guilt, and embarrassment over the past
- Your misconceptions over your self-worth and abilities
- Overcoming procrastination that is related to social anxiety
- Being more realistic and confronting perfectionism

During your CBT process, it may feel like a student-teacher relationship, with the therapist playing the role of a teacher. The concepts will be outlined, and the therapist will help you on your path to change and self-discovery. Also, you will be assigned homework that is crucial to your progress.

Keys to Success in CBT

According to research, there are different keys to success in CBT for social anxiety disorder. The possibility of CBT helping you depends greatly on your expectation of success, your ability to face discomforting thoughts, and your willingness to complete your homework assignments.

Patients who have the zeal to work hard and are positive that CBT offers help, have a higher chance to succeed. Though, the CBT is an intensive therapy that needs active participation from the patient. In the end, the improvement will be long-lasting and worth the hard work.

CBT Methods

Cognitive Behavioral Therapy consists of different techniques, of which many focus on problematic thinking. The cognitive methods help patients lessen the anxiety they feel in interpersonal relationships and in social situations. CBT promises to give patients of social anxiety disorder a feeling of control over how they feel in social situations.

The fundamental goal of CBT is to change your core beliefs, which influence the way you interpret your environment. Changing those core beliefs will lead to a long-lasting recovery from your social anxiety symptoms.

A crucial problem CBT focuses on is the presence of automatic negative thoughts patients of social anxiety disorder have, and the automatic negative ways of thinking that are often twisted with their reality, likely increase their anxiety and reduce their coping ability. These thoughts automatically take place when they think of any anxiety-provoking situation.

For instance, people with the fear of making new friends will elicit thoughts of failure and embarrassment anytime they think of the situation. The aim of CBT is to replace such cognitive distortions with a more realistic view.

At one point in your life, someone has probably told you always to think positively when in situations that trigger anxiety. Sadly, it isn't that easy to do; if it were, a lot of people would've resolved their anxiety issue long ago! Since your brain has been hardwired over time to have anxious and negative thoughts, it will need time to start thinking in a new way. Simply telling yourself, "I will handle the situation better and be less anxious" won't work, based on how you are thinking.

To change your automatic negative thinking for the long-term, you will need to practice every day for several months. Initially, you will be asked to catch your negative thoughts and make them logically neutral. This will later become easier as you work your way up to realistic thoughts. Then it becomes automatic and habitual.

After a while, your memory processes will be affected, and the neural pathways inside your brain will get altered. You start thinking, acting, and feeling different, but with patience, practice, and persistence, progress will be made. Initially, it is a conscious process, but with constant practice and repetition, it becomes an automatic process.

Behavioral Methods

Systematic desensitization is one of the commonly used behavioral techniques to treat social anxiety disorder. It is a type of exposure training that requires your exposure to anxiety-provoking situations to elicit less fear over time.

The exposure training for SAD is always a gradual process. Any exposure training without a gradual step-by-step process will only do more damage than good. Your anxiety will get worse, as you remain in a vicious cycle, which will eventually lead to depression.

With the help of a CBT therapist, you are gradually exposing yourself to social situations that make you anxious so that they will no longer elicit fear. For a start, you can practice imagined exposure by using role playing to practice for a job interview, giving a speech, or introducing yourself to a stranger. Once your imagined and practiced situation gets easier, you can move to the situation in real life. Exposure training moving too fast, or if the situations are too demanding, can go wrong.

Internet CBT for SAD

Providing Cognitive behavioral therapy over the Internet (i-CBT) is gaining popularity and becoming more and more common. Some research supports its use, especially when supported by a professional in mental health.

Since CBT follows a strictly structured format, it is suitable for online applications, consisting of therapy supported interventions or self-help. For patients with severe anxiety who find it difficult to leave the comfort of their home and attend therapy appointments in person, this form of CBT is helpful, too.

We need to use all the cognitive strategies at our disposal, strengthen our resolve to be persistent and consistent in therapies, and make use of all forms of experimental or behavioral activity that will help us manage our social anxiety disorders.

Just like with cognitive therapy, experiments or behavioral activities need to be detailed and comprehensive. The therapist needs to have a list of several behavioral activities that give the patient confidence and peace as they work on the activities.

Finally, for effective and successful treatment of anxiety, behavioral and cognitive therapy needs to be thorough and comprehensive. Reinforcement needs to be a continuous process, and the person needs to be motivated enough to stick to the thirty-minute a day practice routine.

CBT is not the path of lesser resistance for either the patient or the therapist. However, it is the most effective way to surmount social anxiety disorder. The majority of people with a social anxiety disorder will agree to work hard and diligently undertake their therapy, they will tell you they are highly motivated, ready and willing because the work they have to do is nothing when compared to the daily nightmares they had to endure while living with social anxiety.

Having SAD is never easy; it is an everyday struggle and many people hide in denial. Seeking help for it shows you are willing to make progress and remove the shackles of fear. It is this hope of making progress and eventually attaining success that keeps you focused with a positive mind while you proceed forward, aiming for your ultimate goal – freedom!

FINAL WORDS

Social anxiety and all of the other issues that come with it can be difficult to manage. But I strongly believe that with all we've discussed, you have come to understand where your anxiety comes from and how you can nip it in the bud. The fact that you have read this book shows how hungry you are to eliminate social anxiety and achieve social confidence. That is a good thing, but it doesn't stop at just reading.

Don't just read this book and hide away in your comfort zone. The best way to eliminate social anxiety is to be in a social setting. No matter the number of books you read or courses you take, it still boils down to your effort and your discipline to put what you have read into practice. In every section of this book, I have given you well-researched solutions that have worked wonders for myself and countless others. It is my sincere desire that you obtain the same result.

As a way of refreshing the key concepts in this book, let's go over the chapters we've discussed. We opened our discussion with the subject matter "social anxiety." I explained what it means, the types, the likely causes, how you can know if you have it and so on. The purpose was to help you know everything about your problem because there is no way you can combat it without fully knowing it.

From there, we became more specific with our discourse on social anxiety. We looked at when it happens, what it feels like, the core cues that trigger it. We also looked at the physical, behavioral, and emotional symptoms you can experience whenever it happens. I included that chapter to further reiterate that countless people, including myself, know everything you are going through. It is not unique to you and you alone. However, most of those people, including myself, have weathered the storm and eliminated those symptoms so we can live the lives we deserve.

From there, we attacked social anxiety. I gave you several tips that you can adapt in your fight against social anxiety. In that chapter, I made it clear that avoiding social situations is not the solution. The solution is confronting your fears and working your way through it. I gave you tips you can use, including changing your perspective on the issue, avoiding negative coping strategies, and being compassionate with people around you. Let me emphasize that none of the tips in that section were included thoughtlessly. All of them are tips that have been studied by psychologists, and they all proved to be effective against social anxiety. Be kind to yourself and use them.

Then we moved our discussion deeper into how you can go beyond managing social anxiety to overcoming it, like countless others before you. We said that the first thing you should do is to identify the fears and thoughts that fuel your social anxiety. I identified some fears, such as, "they won't like me," "I'm probably going to embarrass myself," and so on. I went on to show you how you can begin to analyze and challenge those fears. Because, trust me, oftentimes, these fears are unfounded, and through logical evaluation, you can start to see this for yourself. In that chapter, we identified some thought patterns that escalate your social anxiety. For example, mind-reading, fortune-telling, catastrophizing and personalizing. Then we said instead of spending your time and energy on those destabilizing thought patterns, you should shift your focus to others instead. I showed you how you could start adopting the social anxiety ladder and a pro-socializing lifestyle as a way of helping your condition.

Sometimes, social anxiety can pile so much pressure on you, that if not managed, you can degenerate into an anxiety attack. I listed some relaxation techniques that can help you calm your nerves whenever you feel your heart beating against your chest. We discussed techniques such as diaphragmatic breathing, autogenic training, progressive muscle relaxation, and guided imagery. I told you the importance of practicing these relaxation techniques, even when you are already relaxed, so that you can easily execute them whenever anxiety is upon you.

The next chapter dealt with yet another problem found with us socially-challenged people, and that is the issue of people-pleasing. I opened that chapter by showing you the signs that tell you are a people pleaser so you don't mistake it for being kind. Then I gave you steps to overcome it, like starting small, giving yourself time, validating and loving yourself.

Then we looked at shyness, its effects, and how to overcome it. We also looked at ways you can begin to build good social confidence and improve your self-esteem. I included that chapter because it is the lack of these attributes that cause social anxiety in the first place. We saw how we could eliminate social anxiety by boosting our social confidence and self-esteem.

We closed the book by discussing the use of therapy for treating social anxiety. We looked at the signs that therapy might be necessary, as well as key therapies like cognitive-behavioral therapy (CBT) and role-playing.

One thing I want you to take away from this book is that social anxiety, shyness, people-pleasing, and lack of social confidence are a bad place to be in your life, but fortunately for you, you can do something about it. You have already started doing so by buying and reading this book. I hope that you will make a conscious effort to see it to the end. Don't just read this book and add it to the collection of books on social anxiety. Read it, and take action.

See you on the social side of life, the part where everything is happening… Good luck!

RESOURCES

ADAA. (2019). *Social Anxiety Disorder.* Retrieved from Anxiety and Depression Association of America: https://adaa.org/understanding-anxiety/social-anxiety-disorder

Albono, A. M. (2014, August 12). *When young people suffer social anxiety disorder: what parents can do.* Retrieved from CareForYourMind: http://careforyourmind.org/when-young-people-suffer-social-anxiety-disorder-what-parents-can-do/

Bhandari, S. (2019, May 20). *What Is Social Anxiety Disorder?* Retrieved from WebMD: https://www.webmd.com/anxiety-panic/guide/mental-health-social-anxiety-disorder#2

Cohut, M. (2019, August 30). *4 top tips for coping with social anxiety.* Retrieved from https://www.medicalnewstoday.com/articles/326211.php#1

Cuncic, A. (2019, November 26). *How to Practice Progressive Muscle Relaxation.* Retrieved from Verywellmind: https://www.verywellmind.com/how-do-i-practice-progressive-muscle-relaxation-3024400

Daskal, L (2017) *9 Simple Ways to Boost Your Self-Esteem Quickly.* Retrieved from https://www.inc.com/lolly-daskal/19-simple-ways-to-boost-your-self-esteem-quickly.html

Felman, A. (2018, February 5). *What's to know about social anxiety disorder?* Retrieved from MedicalNewsToday: https://www.medicalnewstoday.com/articles/176891.php#what-is-social-anxiety-disorder

Griffin, T. (2019, October 6). *How to Be Socially Confident.* Retrieved from WikiHow: https://www.wikihow.com/Be-Socially-Confident

Lo, M. (2019). *5 Ways to Start Building Social Confidence Today.* Retrieved from Lifehack: https://www.lifehack.org/372358/5-ways-start-building-social-confidence-today

Luna, A. (2020, January). *People-Pleasing: The Hidden Dangers of Always Being "Too Nice".* Retrieved from Lonerwolf: https://lonerwolf.com/people-pleasing/

Project, G. (2019, October 20). *5 Necessary Tips to Building Social Confidence.* Retrieved from ThriveGlobal: https://thriveglobal.com/stories/5-necessary-tips-to-building-social-confidence-2/

Rube, T. (2020, January 20). *How to Tell if you are a people pleaser.* Retrieved from WikiHow: https://www.wikihow.com/Tell-if-You-Are-a-People-Pleaser

Sani, S. Fathirezaie, Z. & Talepasand S. (2016) *Physical activity and self-esteem: testing direct and indirect relationships associated with psychological and physical mechanisms.* Retrieved from https://www.ncbi.nlm.nih.gov/pmc/articles/PMC5068479/#!po=63.0435

Shanley, D. (2019). *7 Ways to Overcome Shyness and Social Anxiety.* Retrieved from PsychCentral: https://psychcentral.com/blog/7-ways-to-overcome-shyness-and-social-anxiety/

Smith, M. M. Segal, and Shubin, J. (2019) *Social Anxiety Disorder.* Retrieved from https://www.helpguide.org/articles/anxiety/social-anxiety-disorder.htm

Tartakovsky, M. (2018) *6 Ways to Overcome Social Anxiety.* Retrieved from https://psychcentral.com/lib/6-ways-to-overcome-social-anxiety/

ThisWayUp (n.d) *How do you feel shy.* Retrieved from https://thiswayup.org.au/how-do-you-feel/shy/

Reachout.com (n.d) *10 tips for improving your self-esteem.* Retrieved from https://au.reachout.com/articles/10-tips-for-improving-your-self-esteem

YOUR FREE GIFT

Thank you again for purchasing this book. As an additional thank you, you will receive an e-book, as a gift, and completely free.

This guide gives you 14 Days of Mindfulness and sets you on a two-week course to staying present and relaxed. Practice each of the daily prompts to learn more about mindfulness, and add it to your daily routine and meditations.

You can get the bonus booklet as follows:

To access the secret download page, open a browser window on your computer or smartphone and enter: **bonus.derickhowell.com**

You will be automatically directed to the download page.

Please note that this bonus booklet may be only available for download for a limited time.

Printed in Great Britain
by Amazon